# THE PARTY SYSTEM

*To the valiant men and women who have taken up
the torch of the Social Kingship of Christ, of the coming
New Christendom: know that the lies and calumnies of the
Craven and the Corrupt are the true measure of the fear
your actions instill into the withered hearts of these
acolytes of the Anti-Christ. Persevere! So that
His Will be done on Earth as It is in Heaven.*

# THE PARTY SYSTEM

*by*

Hilaire Belloc
&
Cecil Chesterton

*Foreword by Congressman Ron Paul*

*Introduction by Prince Sforza Ruspoli*

Norfolk, VA
2007

The Party System.
Copyright © 2007 IHS Press.
Preface, footnotes, typesetting, layout, and cover design
copyright 2007 IHS Press.

The Party System was originally published in 1911 by Stephen Swift of London. The
spelling, punctuation, and formatting of the original edition have been largely pre-
served. Minor editorial corrections have been made to the text. All rights reserved.

ISBN-13: 978-1-932528-11-4
ISBN: 1-932528-11-3

FRONTISPIECE: The political cartoon in the foreground of the front cover was
drawn by Max Beerbohm in 1913, at the time of the Marconi Scandal. Originally
entitled "Some Ministers of the Crown," it included a caption that read: "Some
Ministers of the Crown, who (monstrous though it seem) have severally some spare
pounds to invest, implore Sir Rufus Isaacs to tell them if he knows of any stock which
they could buy without fear of ultimate profit." Clockwise around Isaacs are: Winston
Churchill, J. E. B. Seely, Herbert Asquith, Sir Edward Grey, Reginald McKenna,
Augustine Birrell, John Burns and L. V. Harcourt. It was reprinted in *The Chesterton
Review*, Vol. XI, No. 3, August 1985.

Library of Congress Cataloging-in-Publication Data

Belloc, Hilaire, 1870-1953.
  The party system / Hilaire Belloc and Cecil Chesterton ; foreword by Ron Paul ;
introduction by Sforza Ruspoli.
    p. cm.
  Originally published: London : S. Swift, 1911. With new fwd. and introd.
  ISBN-13: 978-1-932528-11-4
  1. Political parties--Great Britain--History--20th century. 2. Elections--Great
Britain--History--20th century. I. Chesterton, Cecil, 1879-1918. II. Title.
  JN1121.B45 2007
  324.241--dc22

                                                                    2007038590

Printed in the United States of America.

IHS Press is the only publisher dedicated exclusively to the social teachings of the
Catholic Church.

For more information, contact:

IHS Press
222 W. 21st St., Suite F-122
Norfolk, VA 23517
info@ihspress.com
www.ihspress.com
877-IHS-PRESS

# TABLE OF CONTENTS

"*The liberal doctrine is that individuals govern themselves through representative legislatures; that parliaments possess the proxies of the people, and that the people are really making laws when their so-called representatives are in legislative session. Actually, parliaments have always tended to become oligarchies of politicians and the hirelings of special interests. The modern parliament may be a forum for the clash and compromise of hostile interests, but it is rarely the voice and expression of any general will or general welfare. It does not actually represent the nation so much as it represents the more powerful and assertive individual interests in the nation.*"

—Ross J. S. Hoffman
*The Sign*, 1934

# FOREWORD

URING MY CAMPAIGN for the 2008 Presidential election, someone asked me in an interview why I wasn't running as a Libertarian, as I did in 1988, or on some other third-party ticket. "Unless you're a billionaire," I told him, "you can't even get on the ballot. And how democratic is that?"

Of course this term "democracy" is open to a number of interpretations. I think in our day it has suffered a bit; people no longer think it's worth very much because they have a sense that those who are supposed to practice it don't take it seriously. Indeed, when I first introduced my Voter Freedom Act back in 1999, one of the things that concerned me was this third-party question: just how hard it is for third party candidates to get any access at all to voters, to express their ideas, and give people a real choice at election time. The laws that exist governing how our system works, rather than fostering the genuine participation of people in the process of government, preserve the two-party monopoly over the political system by effectively disenfranchising supporters of third parties and independent candidates. Supporters of the two-party monopoly regularly use ballot access laws to keep third-party and independent candidates off ballots. So this is just one small example of how the machinery of our government works against other political parties, and it is made to work this way not by accident but by the rules and laws put into place by those very individuals who are supposed to be "custodians" and "watchdogs" over our system. And yet the United States Constitution gives Congress the authority to regulate the time, place, and manner of federal elections. Ballot access is one of the few areas where Congress has explicit constitutional authority to establish national standards. So we have no excuse for not having taken care of this problem.

7

But we haven't done so; nor have we done a whole host of other things that we should be doing. So it's no wonder that people have – and have had for a long time – second thoughts about our system as it currently operates. And so far I'm only talking about what Hilaire Belloc and Cecil Chesterton, in their compact but prescient little treatise on The Party System, called "the machinery" of democracy. Indeed, these two English gentlemen hit on something we are frequently in danger of forgetting:

> [v]otes and elections and representative assemblies are not democracy; they are at best machinery for carrying out democracy. Democracy is government by the general will. Wherever, under whatever forms, such laws as the mass of the people desire are passed, and such laws as they dislike are rejected, there is democracy. Wherever, under whatever forms, the laws passed and rejected have no relation to the desires of the mass, there is no democracy (page 25).

If low voter turnout can be attributed to people at large having doubts about the mechanical process alone – i.e., the voting and campaigns and elections and what have you – if they are doubting whether these things really make a difference, what can we say about their confidence in the bigger picture of self-government? What about this "government by the general will" that Belloc and Chesterton talk about? How much sense do we Americans have today that this is a reality?

The sad fact is that if we today have allowed a decline in our vigilance and watchfulness over our precious freedom, our independence, and our right to manage our affairs for ourselves – such that we feel today that government is simply not responsive to the wishes of the average man and woman – the reality is that this divorce between the will of the people and the workings of the "democratic machine" happened a long time ago, and it did so in a country that we can rightly call the nursery of our own democracy: England.

At least this was the contention of Belloc and Chesterton in 1911 when they penned *The Party System*. "In a true representative system," they wrote, the Executive would be responsible to the elected assembly and the elected assembly would be responsible to the people. From the people would come the impulse and the initiative. They would make certain demands; it would be the duty of their representatives to give expression to these demands, and of the Executive to carry them out (page 26).

The two were convinced that such conditions "did not prevail" in the England of their day, and those of us who wonder just how much they prevail here today would do well to listen to their diagnosis of the disease that they saw plaguing early 20th-century England and its democracy. "Instead of the Executive being controlled by the representative assembly," they observed,

> it controls it. Instead of the demands of the people being expressed for them by their representatives, the matters discussed by the representatives are settled not by the people, not even by themselves, but by the "Ministry"–the very body which it is the business of the representative assembly to check and control (pages 26–7).

Of course American readers may wish to substitute "Cabinet officials" for "the Ministry." There will be other notable divergences of the American system from the pure parliamentary one discussed by the authors of the following text, but the similarities, I believe, will swamp those differences. I'll give several examples.

In general terms, the complaint against the "two-party system"* is given as follows (and doesn't this sound relevant today?):

> ...there is a section of the public, not perhaps large, but certainly increasing, which is beginning to be uneasy about the Party System. It is natural to men to wish to have voice in the government of their native land, and many are beginning to feel that

---

* This is defined by the authors on pages 27–8 as "that method of government in which the representatives of the people are divided into two camps which are supposed to represent certain broad divergences of opinion. Between these two the choice of the election lies, and the side which secures the largest measure of support forms a Government, the minority undertaking the work of opposition." The similarity of this mechanism to our system today needs little comment.

they have no such effective voice today. Laws which they detest are passed, passed easily by the consent of both parties, and they are powerless to defeat or even to protest against them. Measures which they ardently desire and which they know that most of their neighbours ardently desire are never even mentioned. Acts of the Government which seem at the very least proper subjects for criticism and inquiry are suffered without comment. Scandals and blunders of which they have caught a glimpse are suddenly covered over and buried in silence (page 30).

Other examples abound of how similar the Belloc-Chesterton judgment upon the politics of a century ago fits our time. Bruce Fein, associate deputy attorney general under former President Ronald Reagan, was a guest on Bill Moyers' television program this July, denouncing a Congress that he called "invertebrate" in the face of encroachments by our executive branch. An "Executive responsible to the representative assembly" is what Belloc and Chesterton have set forward as the ideal, and yet how many unconstitutional wars, unauthorized wiretaps, signing statements, and foreign renditions do we have to have before this representative body—the Congress—flexes its muscle and takes a stand upon matters of law and our Constitution?

Why does it seem that we in Congress keep moving in the wrong direction, toward further surrender to the Executive? There may be several reasons. Many in Congress are cowed by the campaign funds, the political action committees, the pressure of fundraising, and the threat that can be brought to bear by various pressure groups of a vigorous effort to get one's opponent elected. The parallel to this in the work that follows is Section IV—"The Secret Funds." Money made the political machine go in those days too, and the best that Belloc and Chesterton could do—given the veil of secrecy hanging over what they called the "two huge war-chests" available for the two major parties of the day—was to say that these funds

are subscribed by rich men who want some advantage, financial or social, from the Government, and that they are spent in paying the expenses of members of Parliament—in other words, in corrupting the legislature (page 76).

The ultimate effect of the working of these funds is precisely that of our modern election campaign fundraising and political action and lobbying schemes, with all the potential for abuse and corruption that they mutually entail:

> The effect of paying a man's election expenses out of a secret fund at the disposal of the party organisers is that the member becomes responsible not to his constituents, but to the caucus which pays him. If he opposes some fad of the party organisers or their paymasters, however popular his attitude may be with the electors, the governing gang will find a way to get rid of him, either by the withdrawal of funds, by pressure on the local organisation, or, if all other methods fail, by running an official party candidate against him (page 77).

How familiar this sounds!

The parallels to our time abound; example after example could continue to be put forward to show just how both forward-looking and relevant Chesterton and Belloc were in their denunciation of the two-party monopoly a century ago. The press comes in for a fair criticism, for instance, and its role in campaigns and politics today is, in many regards, as shabby as it was when Belloc was in parliament circa 1910. To remedy the evils of the Party System, the authors write, it is necessary to deal with one of "the most important factors in that life: the influence of the daily Press" (page 144). Though it was admitted, or imagined, at the time, that the influence of the press in England was "peculiar to [that] country," even a casual observer will be struck by the description of Belloc and Chesterton, and how they uncannily seem to be writing about our own time. The characteristics of the press were (and are!):

> the predominance of a very few great daily newspapers, the urban life in which alone the mere suggestion which they represent could have such power, the immense sums necessary to found and to conduct one, the anonymity of the opinions and information they impose and convey (page 144).

The age-old "chicken and egg" question arises here in their treatment of the relationship between the press and the party machinery. Is it the system that pressures the press into supporting the manipulated "drama" of two-party governance? Or is it the press which of its own accord props up this system, and is thus the better object of our criticism and reform?

Aside from the "party funds" that come in for a skewering in Section IV of the Party System, the whole problem of money runs throughout the book as an ultimately corrupting influence in party politics. A final example of this is the Belloc-Chesterton sketch of "the Placeman," someone whom we aren't familiar with, by name, in the American system, but whose description is familiar enough: "the man who enters politics as a profession with the object of obtaining one of the well-paid offices in the gift of the Ministry." No matter what the nature of his activity is, "he will never hint," the authors write, "at existence of things inconvenient...to the Party System as a whole, for on this system he proposes to fatten" (page 43). How common this is today I will let the reader decide; the routine and frequent calls for our elected representatives to concern themselves more with the nation and less with their pocketbooks and reelection might just indicate how far things have gone, in the same direction as these gentlemen sketched a century ago.

They went so far, in fact, as to maintain that the negative influences then at work "reverse[d] the working of the representative machine, turning into an engine of oligarchy what was meant to be an organ of democracy" (page 27). My own continuous sponsorship, now for many years, of the Federal Reserve Board Abolition Act, can be seen in this same light, as a demand for the end of the manipulation of the money supply which sacrifices the interests of the average American, by eroding their standard of living and applying a hidden tax on their dwindling savings, to those of big-spending politicians and well-connected elites, who, respectively, use the Fed's policies to hide the true costs of the welfare-warfare state and obtain access to artificially inflated money and credit before the inflationary effects of those policies impact the rest of us.

Hilaire Belloc and Cecil Chesterton said that they wrote their book in 1911 because even at that time "the game" was not just "farcical, but perilous." They attempted to capture, articulate, and explain the "dim suspicion" that had begun to arise in the minds of at least a section of the people... that the electors do not as a fact control the representatives, and that the representatives do not as a fact control the Government, that something alien has intervened between electors and elected, between legislature and Executive, something that deflects the working of representative institutions (page 27).

What we need are those who, to use the comment Bruce Fein made recently, "say that the country is more important than my party"; those who would put the Constitution and true representative government ahead of mere "political fallout."

Some might be forgiven for thinking the system is too far gone for such individuals ever to make a difference. But I happen to believe that if we are willing to educate ourselves and others, we can restore the kind of government our Founders envisioned. It might be an uphill, even an intimidating and seemingly impossible task. But our work has at least been made easier by these perceptive observations from two of the greatest English writers of last century.

Congressman Ron Paul
Washington, D.C.
October 11, 2007
Maternity of the Blessed Virgin Mary

*"All the odds are on the man who is, intrinsically, the most devious and mediocre—the man who can most easily (and) adeptly disperse the notion that his mind is a virtual vacuum. The Presidency tends, year by year, to go to such men. As democracy is perfected, the office represents, more closely, the inner soul of the people. We move toward a lofty ideal. On some great and glorious day, the plain folks of this land will reach their heart's desire at last, and the White House will be adorned by a downright moron."*

—H. L. Mencken,
*Baltimore Sun*, 1920

# INTRODUCTION

## A Timely Warning from the Past:
## Make Democracy Democratic

EMOCRACY, RECALLING AN APPOSITE if provocative phrase of the French Catholic philosopher Georges Bernanos (replying to a question posed by transalpine anti-fascist students who, in 1946, had invited him to the University of the Sorbonne in Paris), "is the most screwed up word in the world." It is used to say nothing both by professional proponents of "values" and by those pushing anti-values; by idealists and by pragmatists; by conservatives and by revolutionaries; by politicians and by intellectuals; by journalists and by businessmen. In short, it is used to say everything and to say nothing. And frequently – too frequently – it is used to contradict democracy itself. It is a fraud, a clever deception to conceal and to mask the true nature of even authoritarian systems, veiled despots, and the unrestricted power of a handful of parties or lobbies.

If we confine ourselves merely to events of recent years, we will discover "democracy" according to many different models. There is the example of that "Europe" resulting from the encounter between religious tradition and that of secular illuminism, stemming from the conflict between State and Empire. The fruit of the ideological struggles of the nineteenth century and the syntheses of the twentieth century, it has brought forth, on the one hand, and "in the name of the New Man," utopias, dreams, illusions, and messianic fervor; and on the other, concentration camps, gulags, and world wars.

Then there is the "third world" model which has brought to power – democratically, be it noted – fundamentalist forces and leaders, or followers of Fidel Castro, and these because of several grave errors in the foreign policy of the United States.

And then there is the American model, which aims at universalizing and exporting its own conception of democracy, which necessarily reflects "biologically" its own origins and traditions: that is to say the Constitution, which before the French Revolution, had built a State "according to God and according to Reason." This metaphysical conception has encouraged the Americans, independently of their legitimate role in international geo-politics (we are speaking of the Cold War with its opposing blocs of America and the Soviet Union), to believe that the mere spread and functioning of democratic structures – such as elections and parliamentary representation – will bring about naturally the very same democracy by magic (the mysticism of the democratic form). This viewpoint forgets, however, that each people must travel its own road, whether gradually or rapidly, according to its own peculiarities and its own traditions and identity; and that democracy is an historical process, not an ideological one. One cannot invent it (like Jacobinism), nor export it ready-made.

Not only the Ancient Greeks reflected upon and outlined all the possible developments in the sphere of natural politics: democracy which degenerates into dictatorship, aristocracy which degenerates into oligarchy, monarchy into tyranny. Alexis de Tocqueville was not alone in foreseeing the anomalies which might arise in the American democratic system, but was joined by two European intellectuals, the Anglo-Frenchman, Hilaire Belloc, and the Englishman Cecil Chesterton who, in 1911, had taken apart the English and Western model. Bringing together profound analysis and cogent summaries, demonstrating an extraordinary clarity of purpose, and pinpointing the bonds to be broken down so as "to make democracy ever more democratic," they destroyed the ideological lies and exposed the reality of political manipulation as well as the many other related issues which from time to time imprison democracy. Such are the chosen ruses of a governing class that seeks to deceive peoples and manufacture consent. This new edition of *The Party System* is therefore a significant event.

Their work is of remarkable relevance today, for it deals with themes almost prophetically, all the more so given that it was written at the beginning of the twentieth century, when the evil fruits of certain kinds of democracy were not known.

"Votes, elections, and representative assemblies" – stress Belloc and Chesterton in black and white – "are not democracy; they are at best machinery for carrying out democracy." These are words dealt with at length and which stress the correct relationship that should link the form and content of consent, the form and content of representation, as well as between the criteria for organizing society and the democratic values upon which politics is built. Comments and criticisms are made which recall the perennial question: doubts concerning mechanical or quantitative democracy, versus qualitative democracy based on authentic values; about the restricted rights conceded by the System, versus the real needs and interests of the people.

It is no accident that the two intellectuals seek to answer the pivotal question of democracy in their own way: "If Laws are not always consistent with the wishes of the people, is it enough for a simple majority to decide what is just on the moral plane?"

These are historically important questions, to which an exhaustive and definitive answer has still not been given. And so, direct democracy – the direct election of the executive leadership of the State – which was introduced into several parliamentary systems (France and America, for example), has still not gained recognition by everyone so as to be a generally accepted alternative.

Consequently, Belloc and Chesterton go into more depth about the concept of delegation, which goes back to the ideological and political pillars of the liberal, parliamentary, and representative State. Delegation asserts itself – says *The Party System* – "because pure democracy is possible only in a small community." Delegation, therefore, becomes necessary to govern large and complex societies, but it risks losing its usefulness and effectiveness precisely at that moment when the System – the oligarchical, economic, profiteering, financial, and banking party – begins to construct itself. Clearly, Belloc and Chesterton already had the "party-ocracy" and the lobby in mind. In a word, they foresaw the great evil of our democratic modernity, the evil that caused the degeneration of Western society in the twentieth century.

They seek to resolve this problem with proposals which have the outstanding merit of having anticipated the times: "There must be complete freedom in the selection of representatives; the representatives must be strictly responsible to their constituents and to no one else; the representatives must be absolutely independent of the Executive." "Conditions," as they observed, "that do not prevail in England today [1911]." These proposals and background facts, through dissecting the English model, possess their own instructive objectivity. These proposals and background outline the shape of a bottom-up democracy of medieval lineage: a genuine liberty, real power for the people, self-governing communities, effective accountability of the elected by the electors. They would also dismantle, culturally, the Party bureaucracies, and defend the elected representatives' right to freedom of expression and conscience (as prescribed in the Italian Constitution, where representatives are empowered to represent the nation as a whole without particular obligation to those who elected them). And they would provide for a clear separation of powers, creating the conditions for placing effective limits upon government institutions (a step towards "Presidentialism," meaning a special concentration of wide-ranging powers in the person of the President).

In effect, the Middle Ages, which were not a dark age, would be rediscovered. This Age gave people political structures and extremely valuable models and conditions for the organization of society and of the economy, which, if acted upon, might once again today be of immense assistance to contemporary lawmakers. It is surely enough to recall the real freedom enjoyed under the Guild System, and the idea of the authentic, communitarian village, where inequality and natural hierarchies – in the world of arts and crafts – were harmonized perfectly by religious, political, and military unity. The very same traditional England built up an authentic example of democracy worth exporting (this, yes!), founded upon a just balance between the power of the King, an unwritten constitution developed by tradition and custom, and the House of Lords (composed of the aristocracy, guaranteeing the stability of the State) acting as a check upon the House of Commons, which was the expression of a civil reality, but was sometimes a hostage to, or source of, division and ideological collapse.

In Italy, Fr. Luigi Sturzo, the leader of the Popular Party, centered his political struggle upon the need for a grassroots democracy, a genuine democracy. His was an historical battle for proportional representation against the tyranny of parties graced with a majority, and against influential figures and lobbies that were poisoning and polluting democracy. His was an historical struggle – launched at the Congress of Venice in 1921 – in favor of Regions, of local autonomy, of the love of natural community.

Finally, we should not forget the proposal of the minister for telecommunications in the first Berlusconi government (1994) to ensure that lobbies are visible to the public, given that in Italy they are hidden and their interests frequently conflict with the common good. Exactly as has happened in the past, and continues even today in the United States: where parties and politicians choose to defend values and interests of the lobbies, made to appear both legal and transparent in law, while they themselves do not even believe in the "politics of finance" that are based on paper money, globalization, and the excessive power of multi-national corporations and the arms industries.

A Vocational Chamber for the worlds of Work and of Culture, as an independent House, might in the future be a solution to the problem of excessive party influence and the degeneration of democracy, and it might furthermore contribute to forming and choosing a new ruling class that does not have its origins solely in the world of parties.

"To make democracy democratic" is the challenge of our "complex modernity." It is a wager that has to be won. Only the Holy Roman Catholic and Apostolic Church, with its spiritual message and its social doctrine, is capable of assisting the citizen-patriot in creating a human-scale economy, and of building a qualitatively superior democracy based on the highest of values.

But the Church must not be left alone in this work. It must be sustained and supported by a widespread civic initiative involving men from the world of ideas, politics, business, and civil society. All of us together must do our duty.

Prince Sforza Ruspoli
Rome, Italy
September 14, 2007
Exaltation of the Holy Cross

# PREFACE

A Word on the Late Election

**T**HE COUNTRY HAS JUST EMERGED from the heat and dust of a General Election. We have heard it proclaimed on all sides that "the Will of the People must prevail!" with slight variations as to the direction in which the Will of the People is to be found. We have seen Mr Lloyd George and Mr Winston Churchill represented on the one hand as patriots confronting a haughty aristocracy (as represented to Mr Churchill by his cousin the Duke of Marlborough), and braving its wrath and hatred, and on the other as a pair of low-born demagogues hallooing on their ragged and illiterate associates to the plunder of the wealthy! While the Conservatives have professed to be convulsed with fear lest Mr Redmond should buy up the whole Liberal Front Bench with the sum of £40,000 (or $200,000, which sounds at once larger and more insidiously wicked), the Liberals have been singing a moving war-song of which two lines run:

> One with us is He who leads us,
> Asquith, God and right!—

Lines which, however open to objection from theologians, must needs be spirit-stirring to those who presumably conceive Mr Asquith as leaving his plough or his smithy to lead the stormy democracy whose character and aspirations he in his own person sums up and represents to a great attack upon privilege.

Well, it is over for the present, and a good many of the voters are beginning to look at each other and to wonder what it is all about. The question is not an easy one to answer in regard to any election of the present day; but to those who are not in possession of the key, which it is the aim of this book to give, there is about the election which is just over something particularly mysterious.

In the year 1909 the House of Lords, which had previously mutilated and rejected several bills passed by the Liberal Government, threw out Mr Lloyd George's Budget, thereby forcing an immediate General Election. The Liberal leaders declared that the issue at that election was not only the passage of the Budget, but also the limitation of the Lords' Veto; and Mr Asquith, speaking at the Albert Hall, declared that he would neither assume nor retain office unless he were in possession of guarantees that the Lords' Veto should be limited.

Well, what, happened?

On that pledge Mr Asquith won the election. His team was once more returned to power. He did "assume" office; he did "retail" office. But no "guarantees" were forthcoming, and no attack on the Lords was seriously attempted. Instead, Mr Asquith entered into a "conference" with his alleged political "opponents," and six months were supposed to have been spent in the attempt to accommodate the divergent views of the two Front Benches, and to bridge the "unbridgeable gulf" which one of his humbler salaried followers discovered, in a notable speech, to exist between the views of his uncle on the one hand, and of his first cousin on the other. Then both sides came out explaining with bland smiles that the Conference had failed. Immediately afterwards another election was declared to be necessary, though, as a matter of fact, there was absolutely nothing to vote about, the Bill concerning which the two Houses were supposed to be disagreeing never having been really considered by either of them.

The key to this stage-play is not hard to find. The Conference did not fail. It did exactly what it was intended to do. It saved for a moment the life of the moribund Party System. The failure of the Liberal Government to fulfil the popular mandate in 1906, the Chinese Labour betrayal, the monstrous and unpopular interference with public habit and personal liberty included in the Licensing Bill, the collapse and absorption of the Labour Party, had disgusted most people with party politics, so that, in order to rally their supporters, the old cry of "Down with the Lords!" had to be raised. The cry succeeded in its immediate object, but it placed the Government in an awkward position when a handful of Radicals began to demand the fulfilment of the pledges upon which the election had been won. Hence the Conference; hence the alleged "failure" of the Conference; and, finally, hence the election devised in order to give the Party System "second wind."

But the game is growing a little too transparent, and it has never been quite so transparent as at this election. The resolute refusal of the so-called "Opposition" to attack the really vulnerable points in the record of the Government – especially the breach of Mr Asquith's Albert Hall pledge, – and the determination of both sides to direct the attention of the public to unreal issues, all this must begin to suggest the idea of collusion to the ordinary elector. He does not know all; he does not know that practically every move in the silly and dangerous game is arranged beforehand by the confederates on the two Front Benches. But he is beginning to feel that the fight is unreal.

The object of this book is to support the tendency now everywhere apparent and finding expression, a tendency to expose and ridicule as it deserves, to destroy and to supplant the system under which Parliament, the governing institution of this country, has been rendered null.

We write to show why governments suddenly abandon causes which they have enthusiastically espoused, and why Oppositions tolerate such abandonment and lend themselves to such manoeuvres. The former are less obliged to consider the will of the people than to consult the sense of the Governing Group of which they are for the time the representatives, while the latter are less anxious to overthrow their rivals than to preserve the system which in due course, and by the connivance of those rivals, will bring to them also the opportunities and emoluments of office.

A sincere conviction common to a rapidly increasing number of men that, under the present international and domestic condition of England the game is not only farcical but perilous, has suplied our chief motive.

"The new state must discipline and undertake an ethical and educational mission if it is to avoid becoming a mere paternalistic bureaucracy structured over against a mass of unpolitically-minded people. These must be drawn into the life of the state and given that all-important sense of membership. At the same time that they are taught their obligations to the state, they must be shown the limits of what political authority can actually accomplish for the benefit of the individual and the community. For there are not only things which even the most totalitarian state should not do; there are things it cannot possibly do.

"Only a sound political education and a full subjective incorporation of the masses in the life of the state can accomplish this mission and, at the same time, preserve the essential qualities and values of democracy in the new order of politics now arising. These values represent the greatest moral achievements of Western society, and it need hardly be said that unless they are kept—unless, that is, the new state arises out of the democratic order as a mass conversion to political duties and as a transition from mechanical, individualist democracy to organic, hierarchical, and national democracy—there will not be a new state meeting the needs of a new society, but only the familiar corruption of dictatorship and bureaucracy which is ever the political form of a decaying society."

—Ross J. S. Hoffman
*The Organic State*, 1939

THE PARTY SYSTEM

# I

# THE REPRESENTATIVE SYSTEM

The Idea of Representation

**I**T IS HARDLY NECESSARY HERE to argue the abstract question of democracy. All rational political systems that have ever been tolerated among men have been based ultimately on the expression of the popular will, and at the present time at any rate no party can be found that explicitly denies the doctrine of the people's sovereignty. During the last two elections the two parties were shouting against each other that "the Will of the People must prevail," and the only point in dispute was whether the Will of the People was best represented by the Duke of Sussex or by his son-in-law, the Right Honourable James Blagg.

It may, however, be worthwhile to define exactly what democracy is. Votes and elections and representative assemblies are not democracy; they are at best machinery for carrying out democracy. Democracy is government by the general will. Wherever, under whatever forms, such laws as the mass of the people desire are passed, and such laws as they dislike are rejected, there is democracy. Wherever, under whatever forms, the laws passed and rejected have no relation to the desires of the mass, there is no democracy. That is to say, there is no democracy in England today.

Pure democracy is possible only in a small community. The only machinery which perfectly fulfils its idea is the meeting of the elders under the village tree to debate and decide their own concerns. The size of modern communities and the complexity of modern political and economic problems make such an arrangement impossible for us. But it is well to keep it in mind as a picture of real democracy.

The idea of representation is to secure by an indirect method the same result as is secured directly in such communities. Since every man cannot, under modern conditions, vote on every question, it is thought that a number of men might combine to send a man to vote in their name. Men so selected may then meet and vote, and their decision, if they are faithful representatives of the people, may be taken as the decision of the people.

Under no circumstances would such a system work perfectly. But that it may work tolerably, it is essential that the representatives should represent. The extraordinary capacity of politicians for tying themselves in inextricable knots of confused thinking was never better shown than in the current saying that a representative should not be a mere delegate. Either the representative must vote as his constituents would vote if consulted, or he must vote in the opposite sense. In the latter case, he is not a representative at all, but merely an oligarch; for it is surely ridiculous to say that a man represents Bethnal Green[1] if he is in the habit of saying "Aye" when the people of Bethnal Green would say "No." If, on the other hand, he does vote as his constituents would vote, then he is merely the mouthpiece of his constituents and derives his authority from them. And this is the only democratic theory of representation.

In order that the practice may correspond to it, even approximately, three things are necessary. First, there must be absolute freedom in the selection of representatives; secondly, the representatives must be strictly responsible to their constituents and to no one else; thirdly, the representatives must deliberate in perfect freedom, and especially must be absolutely independent of the Executive.

In a true representative system the Executive would be responsible to the elected assembly and the elected assembly would be responsible to the people. From the people would come the impulse and the initiative. They would make certain demands; it would be the duty of their representatives to give expression to these demands, and of the Executive to carry them out.

It must be obvious to everyone that these conditions do not prevail in England today. Instead of the Executive being controlled by the representative assembly, it controls it. Instead of the demands of the people being expressed for them by their representatives, the matters discussed by the representatives are settled not by the people, not even by themselves, but by the "Ministry" – the very body which it is the business of the representative assembly to check and control.

It will be the main business of this book to inquire what is the force which not only obstructs but largely reverses the working of the representative machine, turning into an engine of oligarchy what was meant to be an organ of democracy.

The detailed causes of this reversal will require some careful analysis; but if the thing which makes representative institutions fail here must be expressed in a phrase, the two words which best sum it up are the "Party System."

## What the Public Thinks

We have just attempted a sketch of representative government as it ought to be, and the English people long believed that they had got, if not quite that, at least a decent approximation to it. It was their boast that without bloodshed or violent severance with the past they had as much of the reality of self-government as the most perfectly planned Republic could have. In what degree this was ever true will form the matter of discussion later. But undoubtedly it was widely believed. Most Englishmen until very lately, if told that they were not self-governing, would have laughed in your face.

But now a dim suspicion has begun to arise in the minds of at least a section of the people that this historic optimism is not quite as true as it looks, that the electors do not as a fact control the representatives, and that the representatives do not as a fact control the Government, that something alien has intervened between electors and elected, between legislature and Executive, something that deflects the working of representative institutions.

That thing is the Party System.

A method of government has grown up in our country under which the representatives of the people are divided into two camps which are supposed to represent certain broad divergences of opinion. Between these two the choice of the election lies, and the side which secures the largest measure of support forms a Government, the minority undertaking the work of opposition.

How this system arose, how it has changed, and how it actually works, will be subjects of future consideration. At present we are concerned with the attitude of the public towards it.

First, it must be said emphatically that the body of public opinion upon which the Party System operates is in the main still honest and public spirited. Not to admit this would be to nullify the effect of all criticism of the evil which we are trying to expose; for, as we are all aware, the theoretic differences at least between policies proposed is considerable, and often corresponds to the difference of schools of political thought; and even if we regard the politician as a mere advocate, he does hold a different brief according to the side of the House on which he sits, and though this brief may be unreal to him, *and though, as it is the object of this book to show, he may have, and probably has, no intention of making it the basis of action,* yet it is often real enough to those to whose support he appeals. Thus a Conservative leader must denounce the land taxes which the body of his followers in the country quite sincerely detest, and though, as they begin to suspect, he has no intention of repealing them, yet it would be childish to question the genuineness of the feelings which he is attempting to exploit.

The Party System, which is a game (and a source of profit) to the politicians, is often a matter of deadly earnest to their honest backers in the country.

There are still very many who believe implicitly and fervently in the reality of the conflict. There are Conservatives who are convinced that the Liberal Government is only prevented from dragging the nation through spoliation to destruction by the noble patriotism of the Conservative opposition. There are Liberals who look on Mr Asquith² and Mr Winston Churchill as the tribunes of a people rightly struggling to be free, confronting with undaunted courage the frowns of a haughty oligarchy. The old lady who, on Mr Gladstone[3] being pointed out to her at the funeral of some public personage, remarked: "Oh, I hope he hasn't come to make a disturbance!" is still with us, and so is the enthusiastic and credulous Radical who believes that Mr Churchill has become an outcast from his order by bravely taking the side of the people.

There is another kind of enthusiast who helps to keep the Party System going. This is the man who earnestly desires some particular measure which one of the two parties has espoused, or (what comes to much the same thing) has an intense repugnance to some measure which the other party has espoused. Thus many men, more or less indifferent to politics generally, think that Tariff Reform will benefit their industry, and accordingly vote for the party that advocates it. Again, a man will often find his particular religion affected by legislation in regard to education or religious establishments, and will support the party identified with his views. To the same class belong the militant teetotalers, and the Irish, to whom nothing matters but the cause of their nationality. Men of this type do not form a very large section of the electorate, but they are of importance at elections, and the politicians have to take them into account.

Finally, there is the mass of ordinary voters, largely indifferent to political problems, yet at times keenly interested in politics. How shall we define their state of mind?

Perhaps the best parallel to the attitude of the general public towards politics is to be found in the Oxford and Cambridge Boat Race.[4] Of the crowds that line the towing path every year from Putney to Mortlake there are few that have ever been to either University, have ever known anyone who has been to either, have even the remotest or most shadowy connection with either. Yet they take sides enthusiastically, and would almost be prepared to shed blood for their "fancy." Note that this is not a mere question of backing your judgment on the merits of the two crews. Not one man in ten knows anything about that, and many are proud of always sticking to the same side year after year, of being always

"Oxford" or "Cambridge," whether their favourite colour wins or loses. And just as they vehemently take sides with a University to which they have never been, so they take sides as vehemently with a party which they do not control and from which they can never hope for the smallest benefit.

Such are the mass of the supporters of either party. They derive their political opinions originally from some family tradition or some fanciful preference, but they back them with all the passion of sportsmen. In a vague subconscious way they know it is a game, but they happen to enjoy playing the game.

Nevertheless, there is a section of the public, not perhaps large, but certainly increasing, which is beginning to be uneasy about the Party System. It is natural to men to wish to have voice in the government of their native land, and many are beginning to feel that they have no such effective voice today. Laws which they detest are passed, passed easily by the consent of both parties, and they are powerless to defeat or even to protest against them. Measures which they ardently desire and which they know that most of their neighbours ardently desire are never even mentioned. Acts of the Government which seem at the very least proper subjects for criticism and inquiry are suffered without comment. Scandals and blunders of which they have caught a glimpse are suddenly covered over and buried in silence.

And along with the discontent engendered by these things goes an intangible suspicion that they are in some way the victims of a conspiracy. Why, asks such a man, does not his own side follow up its advantages? Why do his leaders unexpectedly spare their opponents at the very moment when these appear to be in their power? How many honest Radicals were bewildered when the Liberal leaders joined with their rivals to stifle the inquiry into the Jameson Raid![5] How many honest Unionists have been puzzled by Mr Balfour's[6] hesitations and equivocations in the matter of Tariff Reform! How many on both sides have felt somehow fooled and betrayed when they saw the wild agitation and counter-agitation of last year end in a meaningless "Conference"!

It should be remarked, however, that those of whom we speak are generally very far from realising the full truth of their own suspicions. That something is wrong they instinctively feel. What is wrong they would find very great difficulty in defining. They lay the blame now on one leader, now on another. They hardly yet see that the evil is in the system itself. Thus Radicals will say that Mr Asquith is too Whiggish, that he does not fully enter into the feelings of his party in regard to the House of Lords. They do not realise that the whole Liberal Front Bench is as deeply interested as he in keeping the old game going in accordance with the old rules, and dreads as much as any Tory could dread any violent change which might suddenly alter the conditions and perhaps put a summary end to the contest. Thus, again, enthusiastic Tariff Reformers condemn Mr Balfour as weak. They fail to see that the real difficulty is not that he is weak, but that he is strong – strong in the traditions of party, the complex system of relationships and alliances that cover English politics like a net, much too strong to allow his hands to be forced by the Tory Democracy. Men of all opinions were puzzled, bewildered, and somewhat perturbed by the Conference, not knowing that it was but a more formal type of those thousand private Conferences between opposing leaders behind the Speaker's chair and at dinner parties and social clubs which give their real direction to the politics and to the destinies of modern England.

## Past and Present

It is an error to suppose that the Party System was always the organised imposture which it is today. There was a time when it had a meaning – nay, even within times comparatively recent it meant more than it means now.

During the seventeenth century there was in England a definite conflict of political ideals. The old conception of kingship was at war with the theory of Parliamentary Government; and the vital reality of the struggle was proved by the one infallible test, the fact that men were willing to fight and kill and be killed for their own ideal. The war went on with varying fortunes until the Revolution of 1689, which marked the final triumph of one doctrine over the other.

It is a great though a not uncommon mistake to suppose that that triumph was a triumph of democracy. The Revolution took for its excuse indeed a democratic theory, simply because some excuse of the sort must be taken by anyone who attempts to put his political success upon a moral basis. There is not, and never has been, any moral theory of sovereignty conceivable that was not based upon the ultimate sovereignty of the community. But neither in motive nor in practice was there a democratic force behind the Revolution of 1689.

The Revolution of 1689 was not made by the people. The populace of London and of certain prosperous southern towns may have been in favour of it, but the mass of ancient and rural and then numerically preponderant England was certainly against it. The Revolution was made not only by but for a group of wealthy intriguers with an object in the main financial. That group of men and their successors proceeded to enrich themselves at the public expense in every conceivable way. Perhaps the best commentary upon the Revolution of 1689 is to be found in the enclosure during the century and a half which followed the accession of the House of Hanover of more than 6,000,000 acres of common land by the rich landowners and their satellites who had drawn the sword for "civil and religious liberty."

What triumphed in 1689 and again in 1715 and 1745 was not the people but the Parliament. The Parliament did not represent the people; indeed, it hardly professed to do so. It was jealous of any publicity given to its debates, it gloried in the private possession of seats in Parliament by particular magnates, and perhaps the most significant symptom of its character was the comparative efface-ment of the House of Lords.

The Parliament, then, represented a narrow class, which had for its base the great landowners, but for its buttresses the mer-chants, and for its recruitment wealth in any form however got-ten. But it should be remembered that within this class there were real differences of opinion. The political conflicts of the eighteenth century were therefore, compared with our own, real conflicts. The Parliament might have little regard for the mass of the people, but it was powerful as against the mere Executive. The fact that strong Ministers were obliged to spend enormous sums in bribing the legislature proves that the legislature was able to control them, and, if not placated, to overthrow them. Such direct bribery has now ceased, but it may be questioned whether this cessation is not due rather to the growing impotence of the House of Commons than to any increase in public virtue. So again the conflicts of Pitt[7] and Fox[8] had this difference from the conflicts of rival politicians of the present day, that they extended to the sphere of private life. The two men did not speak to each other. They belonged to the same class, no doubt, for it was the only class possessed of any political power. But they did not, like Mr Asquith and Mr Balfour, belong to the same set.

The system of politics which lasted from the beginning to the end of the eighteenth century was finally disturbed by two forces: The material powers created by the industrial revolution and the ideas generated by the Great Revolution of France. The two combined produced the Reform Bill of 1832. New wealth had been created by the new machinery, and this new wealth led to an extension in the class of the newly made rich, which gravely disturbed the old balance between the merchants and the mere landowners. The newly made rich continued to be rapidly and effectually digested into the governing class; indeed, it was Pitt's persistent policy to meet the new situation by a wholesale creation of plutocratic peers; but a sufficient margin of rich men remained outside the organism of the governing class to disturb the equilibrium, and hence the old representative system found itself in direct conflict with masses of the new wealth.

Throughout the first half of the nineteenth century there was something like a real struggle between the commercial and the territorial rich — a struggle that culminated in the fight over free trade. Today, not only has the struggle ceased, but the line of demarcation can no longer be drawn. Nobles and gentlemen of the old territorial class are now deeply interested in commercial speculations of all kinds, not only as urban landlords but as speculators and directors. On the other hand the newly made rich buy landed estates, county seats, and—what is more important than all—permanent legislative power in the House of Lords. At the present day the purchase of legislative power, which is the normal and shameful method of recruitment in the House of Lords, is almost invariably effected by men who have made their fortunes either in commerce or by money-lending. It is rare to find a large landowner who is also a commoner entering the market and purchasing a peerage.

We have today to deal not with a divided but with a united plutocracy, a homogeneous mass of the rich, commercial and territorial, into whose hands practically all power, political as well as economic, has now passed.

During the whole course of the nineteenth century two processes have been going on side by side, the one patent to all the world and the foundation of much comment and speculation, the other almost entirely unobserved and unmentioned.

The first is the extension of the franchise. Step by step since 1832, more and more citizens have been admitted to vote for members of Parliament. First the clerk or shopkeeper, then the urban workman, and finally the agricultural labourer became an elector. This process should clearly have meant an increase in the power of democracy, and it has been practically universally assumed that it did mean this. But in fact it is extremely dubious whether the mass of the people have as much political power today as they had before the process began. Had the enfranchisement of the people come suddenly there is little doubt that something like real democracy would have been achieved. But it came by slow degrees, and there was time for another process to go on side by side with the widening of the franchise.

That process was the transfer of effective power from the House of Commons to the Ministry, or, to speak more accurately, to the two Front Benches, Government and "Opposition." There was no definite moment at which you could say that this was done, but it has been done very thoroughly by now. Anyone who doubts this will find it easy to convince himself of it by glancing at the relations of the House and the Executive at the beginning of the process and at the end. At the beginning the Government was dependent on the House; now the House is in a state of abject dependence on the Ministers and ex-Ministers, who arrange between them details of all policies.

A very simple test will show this. One of the most important historic powers of the House of Commons is the power of driving a Minister or Government from office. That power was not only possessed by the early Parliaments of the nineteenth century, but was continually exercised; and Administrations, strong in reputation and in parliamentary support, were repeatedly overthrown by revolts of their own followers, and dismissed by the vote of the Commons. So Wellington was overthrown in 1830, and Grey in 1834. So Peel was driven from power by the Protectionist revolt in 1845. So Lord John Russell fell in 1852, and so in a few months afterwards fell the Ministry of Derby and Disraeli. So the Coalition Ministry of Lord Aberdeen was defeated in 1855 by a vote of censure on the conduct of the Crimean War. So in 1857 Palmerston was beaten on the Chinese War, and again in 1859 on the Conspiracy Bill. So in 1865 the strong Ministry of Russell and Gladstone was overthrown on its Reform Bill by the rebellion of the Adullamites.[9]

If we take the year 1870 as the pivot year, we shall find that in the forty years that preceded 1870, nine Administrations which could normally command a majority of the Commons were upset by the independent action of members of that House. In the forty years that have passed since 1870 only one instance of this happening can be mentioned – the defeat of Mr Gladstone's Home Rule Bill of 1886. There the circumstances were in many ways exceptional, and even that example is now nearly a quarter of a century old. In the last twenty-four years not a single case of such independent action on the part of the Commons has occurred.

Another illustration, if further illustration be needed, of the progressive emasculation of the House of Commons may be found by comparing its attitude in the matter of the Crimean War waged fifty years ago, and its attitude in the matter of the South African War waged only the other day. Both wars, whether wise or foolish, just or unjust, were undoubtedly supported by the bulk of public opinion both within and without Parliament. Both wars were scandalously mismanaged. But the Crimean War was fought when Parliament was comparatively free. As soon as the details of the mismanagement began to be known in England there was a fierce popular agitation, and the popular voice was immediately heard not only in the Press but also in Parliament. A Committee of Inquiry was demanded and refused. But in spite of the opposition of the men in power the demand was carried in the House of Commons by a huge majority. The result was that Lord Aberdeen had to resign and Lord Palmerston took his place. Palmerston wanted to get rid of the Committee, but the House insisted, and he, powerful and popular as he was, was obliged to bow to its will. All this was done, it must be remembered, not by the Opposition or the Peace Party, but by men returned to support the Government – men who thoroughly approved of the war and merely wished to see it efficiently conducted.

In the case of the South African War there was plenty of grumbling in the country, and not a few sensational exposures of the incompetence and corruption which weakened our arms. But within the walls of Parliament scarcely a voice was heard, and it certainly never entered the head of any Conservative member (or Liberal member either for that matter) to take the strong step of driving out the men in power and putting better administrators in their place. Indeed, the war was conducted invariably without consulting Parliament; and during the whole of its course financial scandals, quite openly talked of among the educated classes of this country, had no place in Parliamentary discussion. The House of Commons had ceased to be an instrument of government.

To whom, then, has the power of the House of Commons passed? It has passed to a political committee for which no official name exists (for it works in secret), but which may be roughly called "The Front Benches." This committee is not elected by vote, or by acclamation, or even by general consent. Its members do not owe their position either to the will of the House or the will of the people. It is selected – mainly from among the rich politicians and their dependents – by a process of sheer and unchecked co-option. It forms in reality a single body, and acts, when its interests or its power are at stake, as one man. No difference of economic interest or of political principle any longer exists among its members to form the basis of a rational line of party division. Nevertheless, the party division continues. The governing group is divided arbitrarily into two teams, each of which is, by mutual understanding, entitled to its turn of office and emolument. And a number of unreal issues, defined neither by the people nor by the Parliament, but by the politicians themselves, are raised from time to time in order to give a semblance of reality to their empty competition.

That is the Party System as it exists today, and by it the House of Commons has been rendered null, and the people impotent and without a voice.

## II

# THE GOVERNING GROUP

The Making of Ministries

INCE WE HAVE SEEN that, during the last century, power has been silently transferred from the House of Commons, it becomes a matter of vital importance to ask to whom it has been transferred. We have already said that it has been transferred to the Cabinet; but what is a Cabinet, and how is it constructed?

The theory of the Constitution is that Ministers are nominated by the Crown. Everyone knows that this has ceased to be the fact. Many people would tell you that now Ministers are in effect nominated by Parliament. But this is equally far from the truth. The plain truth is that Ministers nominate themselves. They form a self-elected body, filling up its vacancies by co-option.

The two Front Benches are close oligarchical corporations; or, to speak more accurately, one close oligarchical corporation, admission to which is only to be gained by the consent of those who have already secured places therein. The price which has to be paid for admission is, of course, a complete surrender of independence, and absolute submission to the will of the body as a whole.

The greater number of the members of this close corporation enter by right of their relationship, whether of blood or marriage, to other members of the group, no matter of what social rank. They may be called the Relations. This family arrangement must not be confused with what once was the old aristocratic privileges of the Great Houses.

There are still indeed certain wealthy political families whose members are regarded as having a prescriptive right to share in the government of the country. Their wealth is more and more important, their lineage less and less.

The traditions of the English political system having been aristocratic in character, render the presence of the members of such families (in lessening degree) antecedently probable; but while the public realises this, it is not aware of the degree in which mere relationship, high or low born, enters into the making of Ministries, still less of the way in which family ties enter into the formation of the two closely connected Front Benches, where there is no question of aristocratic descent.

It is neither novel nor astonishing to discover a Duke of Norfolk acting as Postmaster-General under a Conservative Administration. As the Duke of Devonshire was a member of former governments, so one would imagine that the present Duke, his nephew, would naturally hold office in any future Unionist Administration. The public even expects that Mr Austen Chamberlain should inherit, as it were, Cabinet rank from his father; nor is it much scandalised to see the Prime Minister's brother-in-law, Mr Tennant, sitting by his side on the Treasury bench. Mr Churchill, of course, as a member of the family whose name he bears, and as heir to his father's career, has a double right.

But the list begins to grow long when we see Lord Selborne, the son-in-law of a former Prime Minister, Lord Salisbury, governing South Africa at a moment when his first cousin, Mr Arthur Balfour, is the Prime Minister of the day (being retained there subsequently by Mr Balfour's "opponents"), while that Prime Minister's brother, Mr Gerald Balfour, not only enjoys long years of office through his family connection, but a considerable public pension into the bargain when office is no longer open to him. That Lord Gladstone should inherit from his father may seem normal enough, though his name does swell this extended category. But to find Lord Portsmouth Under Secretary for War, while a cousin of his wife's, Sir John Pease, has yet another post under the present Government, and his cousin again, Mr Pike Pease, the reversion of a "Conservative" post; and to have to add to this that the Liberal Whip, Sir John Fuller, is actually the brother-in-law of the Parliamentary Secretary to the Treasury,

Mr Hobhouse, both being grandchildren by blood or marriage of a Conservative Chancellor, Lord St Aldwyn (Sir Michael Hicks-Beach), touches upon the comic when we remember how large a proportion of the paid offices available this list represents. Nor do the names here jotted down almost at random present more than a very small sample of the whole system.

It must be noted that these family ties are not confined to the separate sides of the House. They unite the Ministerial with the Opposition Front Bench as closely as they unite Ministers and ex-Ministers to each other.

For instance, to quote again chance connections that occur to one, the present talented and versatile ("Liberal") Under Secretary for Home Affairs, Mr Masterman, is the nephew by marriage of the late ("Conservative") Colonial Secretary, Mr Lyttelton; who, in his turn, is closely connected with Mr Asquith, for they married sisters. The present ("Liberal") President of the Council, Lord Beauchamp, is brother-in-law of a former Conservative Governor of Madras, Lord Ampthill; a "Liberal" and a "Unionist" Whip, the two Peases, are cousins (the latter of Ministerial rank, though not of course yet in enjoyment of office); and, as all the world knows, Mr Winston Churchill is not only the cousin of a former Conservative Minister, the Duke of Marlborough, but directly succeeded the head of his own family in the post he held, that of Under Secretary for the Colonies.

Points of this kind are of importance, for they show to how restricted a group of men the functions of government have come to be entrusted. They are effects, not causes, of its narrowness. None can deny that the phenomena are peculiar to a political condition exceedingly abnormal. Groups of this sort could not possibly arise in a genuinely democratic society; and, what is more, are more closely and intricately bound together even than they were in the days when the government of this country was avowedly that of an oligarchy. The tendency to govern by clique is not decreasing; it is increasing.

But, it may be asked, is there anything wrong in men differing in politics yet remaining on friendly terms in private life? Is there any reason why a man should not marry a woman because her family belongs to the political party opposed to his? Not the least in the world. Such things would naturally happen in the most real and earnest political conflict. But they would happen as exceptions; there would be perhaps one or two such cases in every generation. When we find such things not exceptional, but universal, we may safely say that we are not considering a certain number of examples of personal sympathy or attraction over-riding political differences, but a general system of government by a small, friendly, and closely inter-related clique. We are not surprised at Romeo loving Juliet, though he is a Montague and she a Capulet. But if we found in addition that Lady Capulet was by birth a Montague, that Lady Montague was the first cousin of old Capulet, that Mercutio was at once the nephew of a Capulet and the brother-in-law of a Montague, that County Paris was related on his father's side to one house and on his mother's side to the other, that Tybalt was Romeo's uncle's stepson, and that the Friar who married Romeo and Juliet was Juliet's uncle and Romeo's first cousin once removed, we should probably conclude that the feud between the two houses was being kept up mainly for the dramatic entertainment of the people of Verona.

It should further be noted that the kindly tolerance on which politicians are so fond of congratulating themselves is extended only to those who play the game and not at all to those who spoil the game. It was not extended to Parnell. It was not extended to Mr Victor Grayson.[10] It is the result not of magnanimity, but of indifference.

Finally, the mere fact that the electorate is never allowed to learn the full truth as to these relationships and intimacies is sound moral proof that their motive is a motive of imposture.

The second division, and reserve as it were of Cabinet material, may be called the Private Secretaries. Sons of good families, inadequately provided for, sons of the new rich with political ambitions, sons especially of persons who have helped to finance prominent politicians or have subscribed largely to the Party Funds, often obtain positions as private secretaries to the great men on the Front Benches. If they are fairly apt and industrious they have little difficulty in making themselves useful, in rising in the political world, and eventually (sometimes quickly) in obtaining Cabinet rank. Mr

Montagu's career, like that of his cousin Mr Herbert Samuel, has been of this kind. These two related members also touch another part of our subject, for one is the son, the other the nephew, of the late Lord Swaythling, formerly Sir Samuel Montagu.

Finally, there are those whom we may roughly describe as the make-weights–persons having no direct family or financial connection with the ruling group, but co-opted by the Ministers, sometimes because they have made some sort of reputation in the House or in the country, sometimes because they are in possession of some other source of influence which it is thought may be useful to the two Front Benches, sometimes because they have given, and are still capable of giving, annoyance to the Professional Politicians when in an independent position. Clever lawyers are often taken into the service of the oligarchy in this way, and there is at least one well-known case of an ex-workman being so taken. Such men, not feeling sure of their footing, are generally especially pliant to the will of the oligarchy. Commonly they become merged in it. Thus, when Mr Asquith entered the Gladstone Government of 1892, he was, we believe, unconnected by any direct tie with the governing group. Now he and his are connected by a dozen such ties.

It is clear, then, that the method by which Ministries are formed is the method of co-option. No man is made a Minister by election or acclamation either of the people or of the legislature. Office, unlike the kingdom of heaven, is not taken by storm. That a man may enter its narrow gate, he must prove himself able and willing to be a serviceable tool of those who hold the keys. And this power of the oligarchy to admit or refuse Ministerial appointments is perhaps the most powerful means used by them to fetter the House of Commons. Their control over the bestowal of places has created in the House a large class of placemen and placemen-expectant, upon whose interested support the machinery of party discipline largely depends.

The Placemen

The Placeman is a historic figure in English politics. He is as prominent and important a figure at the present time as he was in

Walpole's[11] day. The publication of Parliamentary proceedings and the introduction of a democratic element into the House of Commons have made it necessary to cover his operations with a veil of somewhat greater decency, but his character and functions are in essence just what they always were.

The Placeman is the man who enters politics as a profession with the object of obtaining one of the well-paid offices in the gift of the Ministry. His mode of operation will necessarily vary according to his talents and temperament. Sometimes he will endeavour to earn the gratitude of the governing group by voting steadily according to the dictation of the Whips (a high record in divisions, when it is not a hobby or a method of duping a constituency, may generally be taken as the mark of an embryo or prospective Placeman), by coming to the rescue of the Ministers, and defending them when their followers prove restive, by always being ready to put down "blocking" motions to prevent the discussion of inconvenient topics, or to move "shelving" amendments or inconvenient motions. Sometimes he plays a bolder game, assumes the airs of an independent member, criticises the Government from time to time, asks inconvenient questions, and makes himself a mild nuisance to the Front Benches and the Whips. But by this sign the mere Placeman may always be known that, though he may ask questions or raise matters slightly inconvenient to his "leaders," he will never hint at existence of things inconvenient to *both* Front Benches and awkward to the Party System as a whole, for on this system he proposes to fatten.

The change which office produces in men of this type is often extraordinary. Take the case of Mr C. F. G. Masterman. Mr Masterman entered Parliament as a Liberal of independent views. During his first two years in the House he distinguished himself as a critic of the Liberal Ministry. He criticised their Education Bill. He criticised with especial force the policy of Mr John Burns at the Local Government Board. His conduct attracted the notice of the leaders of the party. He was offered office, accepted it, and since then has been silent, except for an occasional rhetorical exercise in defence of the Government. One fact will be sufficient to emphasise the change. On March 13th, 1908, Mr Masterman voted for the Right to Work Bill of the Labour Party. In May of the same year he accepted a place with a salary of £1200 a year–it has since risen to £1500. On April 20ᵗʰ, 1909, he voted, at the bidding of the Party Whips, against the same Bill which he had voted for in the previous year. Yet this remarkable example of the "peril of change" does not apparently create any indignation or even astonishment in the political world which Mr Masterman adorns. On the contrary, he seems to be generally regarded as a politician of exceptionally high ideals. No better instance need be recorded of the peculiar atmosphere it is the business of these pages to describe.

In the same category we may include the mischief which accompanies the presence of so large a number of barristers in Parliament, where barristers abound, because they always have something to get from the Government. The prizes in this profession are high, and they are all at the disposal of the governing group. Therefore the fairly successful lawyer is always the most serviceable tool of the Ministers. It was a lawyer, Mr Buckmaster, who moved the amendment which shelved the question of the secrecy of the Party Funds. It was a lawyer, or rather two or three lawyers, who were employed to damp down the Nationalist movement in Wales. Indeed, Wales presents a particularly strong case, for the consistent policy of the Government has been to buy off the Welsh by giving promotion to Welsh barristers.

A striking case of the way in which barristers are rewarded is that of Mr Horridge. Mr Horridge defeated Mr Balfour at Northeast Manchester in 1906. It was generally understood that he was to have the first judgeship that fell vacant. When, however, the first vacancy occurred the Education Question was to the fore, and it was felt that a by-election in Manchester would be dangerous. Mr Horridge was therefore passed over, and the place was given to another political lawyer, Mr Hemmerde. When the General Election came, Mr Horridge did not stand again; immediately after it his fidelity was rewarded with the long-expected judgeship. Now Mr Horridge happens to be a good judge. *O si sic omnes!*[12]

There are thus in every House of Commons a very large number of men who either have received or expect to receive places which are in the gift of the Government. On the other side of the House are an almost equally large number who expect to receive places from the next Government as soon as their own party is in power. Between them they make up an important section of the House, and they can be absolutely relied on by Government and Opposition to vote straight as the ruling group direct.

At the same time it must be remembered that the influence which the Front Benches can exert over members of Parliament is by no means confined to those who have places or to the much larger class of those who think they may some day get places. In a thousand ways the position of a man who renders himself obnoxious to the governing group can be made unpleasant; in a thousand ways submission to them can be rewarded by little favours. One member refrains from pressing some inconvenient inquiries on the Foreign Office or the India Office because he is about to take a trip to Egypt or India and wishes to have no obstacles thrown in his way. Another—perhaps a lawyer—will refrain from taking up a determinedly independent attitude because, if he gets the reputation of being "impracticable," it may injure him professionally. Another wants some private Bill in which either he or his constituents are interested to pass smoothly and rapidly. None of these men want to make themselves unnecessarily unpopular with the group in whose hands is not only the disposal of places, but the Executive Government and the absolute control of the time of the House. Add to these considerations the pressure which the Party Caucus can (as we shall see hereafter) exercise upon elections, and it is not surprising that the ancient control of the House of Commons over the Ministry has been replaced by despotic authority of the Ministry over the House of Commons.

There is, of course, a large margin in any House of Commons to whom no direct or conscious pressure can be said to apply. They would themselves be quite genuinely and sincerely astonished if they were told that any pressure was exercised upon them, or that any advantage was held out to them by what they would call "loyalty to their party." They are men, for the most part wealthy, men who regard a seat in the House of Commons as a social honour which they have purchased with a certain expenditure of their money and their energy, men who take the duties of their position seriously, and who perform all that part of parliamentary work which is less touched by corruption adequately and well. They do excellent work upon committees, they busy themselves with the minor details of their constituencies, they speak for hard cases, they try to obtain petty situations for their supporters, etc. These men are perfectly honest, and would be more astonished than any reader of this book, or than any ordinary member of the electorate, to hear that pressure was put upon them by the cynical and happily outworn clique upon which the placemen openly depend for their livelihood.

Now, to the plain citizen the astonishment is not that pressure should be put upon such men, but that they do not recognise the pressure.

The plain citizen will never be persuaded that Mr Brown, young Lord Jenkinson, and Sir James Smith always think in the same way upon all matters. He cannot conceive why they should always vote the same way, unless they have motives as bad and as fraudulent as those of the regular placeman whom they support. It behoves us, therefore, to ask how the contradiction arises, and how perfectly honest men can be made to serve the system?

The main pivot of the machine lies in the fixed custom of dissolving when a majority is expressed against the act of any Minister. True, this capital point of the whole parliamentary game has latterly, with the advent of groups, lost something of its force. But it still survives as a main instrument by which the ordinary and honest member is coerced.

The Government does now and then give way when it appreciates that a majority may possibly be formed against it; and there have been of late years two or three rare and minor instances in which the expression of the popular will through its representatives in Parliament has controlled the Executive—as, for instance, in Clause IV. of the Trades Dispute Bill. But, as a rule, the working of the machine is as follows: The Government, after consultation with the other half of the clique who sit on the Opposition Front Bench, determine that such and such a proposal is their "policy."

If a majority of the House of Commons disapprove by their vote of such a "policy," a General Election, with all its expense of time, energy, and money, is imposed upon every member of the House.

The situation is precisely as though a King (when the Crown had real power) had been able to say to the Commons: "I propose to spend so many millions on an addition to my standing army, and if you express disapproval of this I will fine every man Jack of you a thousand pounds, and imperil his chance of ever coming back to oppose my will!" For it must be remembered that though the party funds are lavishly used to support even the richest members of the party, they are despotically controlled, unaudited, and immediately withdrawn from any member who has voted against the directions of the Government, whose directions are never more emphatic than when they are issued after a consultation with their nominal opponents.

It is this necessity, the necessity of "keeping the Government in," or paying a heavy penalty in money, time, energy, and the imperilling of one's place in Parliament, which controls the great body of men who cannot come under any of the categories we have yet mentioned, and in a later part of this book we will return to the subject when we consider what remedies there may be for the present impasse.

## The Secret Alliance

The popular defence of the elaborate system of indirect corruption described in the last section is that it is necessary for the maintenance of discipline.

Now, discipline is a military term, and implies the existence or prospect of a war. It is obviously inapplicable to matters of legislation, except under most extraordinary circumstances. It is the idea of a good soldier that he obeys the orders of his superior—"His is not to reason why, etc." But it is the very object of the legislator to "reason why." His function is criticism; and discipline is fatal to criticism, and is meant to be so. Soldiers are not there to criticise their officers, but to follow them. Members of Parliament, on the other hand, are there (or ought to be there) to criticise the Ministers; and it is certain that they cannot effectively criticise so long as they obediently follow.

There is only one possible occasion upon which the word discipline could ever properly be applied to Parliamentary affairs, and that would be some momentous crisis (such as only occurs once in two or three centuries) when politics begin really to take on the aspect of civil war or revolution. No one will pretend that such a state of things exists at the present time. But there are still a good many people who believe the conflict between the two parties to be, as far as it goes, a real one. Young Liberals are told that they must drop minor differences that they may present a serried front to the forces of reaction. The Conservative rank and file have it impressed upon them with equal emphasis that their enforced unity is the only obstacle to a devastating flood of confiscatory revolution.

Now, if we were soldiers in an army subjected to a system of military law of unusual severity, we should perhaps submit cheerfully to our lot so long as we believed in the vital reality and value of the cause for which we were fighting. But, if we found that all the time that we were being flogged or shot for the smallest infraction of discipline, our chief officers were continually conferring with the officers of the enemy, were on the best of terms with them, concocted their plan of campaign in concert with them, always carefully avoided every occasion of decisive engagement between the two armies, and generally treated the whole war as a friendly game of mixed chance and skill between themselves and their friends and relations on the other side,–then I think our floggings and shootings would justly become a matter for complaint and even for mutiny.

That is, briefly, the political situation today. On the rank and file is imposed a rigid discipline which nothing but an extraordinary public crisis could justify, while at the same time the commanders treat the whole affair as the most frivolous of amusements, the keen enjoyment of which need in no way disturb the friendliness of their private relations. That is the situation, and it is becoming to most of us an intolerable one.

The recent "Conference" of eight members of the governing group to discuss the question of the House of Lords opened the eyes of a good many people who were previously blind to the unreality of the struggle. It was a little too impudent! Yet behind the irony of this silent compact coming after all the heroic rhetoric of the General Election there was a deeper irony. The ordinary journalistic picture of the conference suggests that Mr Asquith and Mr Balfour met for the first time, bowed to each other with cold civility, and proceeded to discuss terms of settlement with the polite hauteur of dignified enemies. As a matter of fact, of course, this Conference, trumpeted through the press as if it were a unique event, was only one of the hundred conferences which various members of the two Front Benches, and especially the two leaders, their secretaries, the two Chief Whips, the confidential hangers-on, and now and then the principal official paymasters habitually hold to settle the affairs of Parliament. Agreement between the Front Benches is not a rare expedient suited to a special crisis. It is the normal method of governing the country.

We spoke just now of the generals as carefully avoiding the possibility of any decisive engagement between their followers. Anybody who recalls what has happened during the last twenty years can remember repeated cases where one side seemed on the point of achieving a decisive victory over the other, when a halt was suddenly called, the troops ordered back to quarters, and the battle abandoned. A subject is raised. It forms the topic of numerous and heated orations. The country is wildly excited about it. Then it is suddenly dropped; nobody knows why–except the Front Benches.

A very strong case may be found in the Committee of the House of Commons which inquired into the Jameson Raid. It will be remembered that that Committee seemed always on the very verge of some startling revelation, but that just at the sensational moment the inquiry–like a newspaper serial–abruptly stopped. Now, it is obvious that, if the fight between the parties were a genuine one, there was nothing more to be desired by the Liberal members of the Committee than an exposure which might have discredited the Ministers in power. Yet Sir William Harcourt[13] and Sir Henry Campbell-Bannerman,[14] and their henchman, Mr Ellis, were as eager as any Tory could be to hush up anything that might discredit the Colonial Office. Why was this? Because they also were Front Benchers, and at all times of crisis the Front Benches hang together.

Another case was that of Chinese Labour.[15] If ever an election was won on a specific issue, the election of 1906 was won on Chinese Labour. This is not the place to express an opinion on the merits of the question; we simply state the facts. If the representatives of the people had acted according to their instructions, the repatriation of the Chinese would have begun at once and upon the largest possible scale. Everybody knows that this was not done; on the contrary, anxious negotiations were entered into by the Ministry to propitiate the South African Jews, a common plan was agreed on between the two Front Benches and those magnates, and 1300 Chinese were admitted to the Rand after the change of Government. But this is not the important point. The important point is that the new House of Commons, elected mainly on that issue, *was not allowed to divide on the question or to express any opinion upon the policy which should be adopted.* But we shall return to this capital and decisive illustration in more detail upon a later page.

A third example may be found in the recent "Conference." Who, listening to the torrents of eloquence poured out during the last General Election, to the Liberal fulminations against the tyranny of the Lords, to the Unionist fulminations against the "Socialism" of the Liberals, to Mr Balfour's denunciations of Mr Ure, and to Mr Ure's retorts on Mr Balfour, to the repeated appeals of both sides to the Voice of the People, would have believed that the whole tragic business was to be openly branded as a farce by its very authors, or that these gentlemen would indulge in sham secret meetings, which, even had they pretended to reality, would have been a negation of all that had been said and done five months before?

But if, from a past which is known, we turn to a future which may be confidently predicted (for accurate prediction is the best of all tests that can be applied to theory), we have an immediate example before us.

The moment at which this book appears offers an opportunity for putting its thesis to the test.

It has been determined by the two Front Benches to alter both the Constitution and the powers of the House of Lords. In what way will those powers be altered, and what body will take the place of the present Second Chamber?

Without any reasonable doubt, the powers of the House of Lords, after the most ridiculous sham demagogy from the Treasury Bench, and equally ridiculous sham indignation from their relatives and private friends across the table, and after perhaps some sham resistance organised to give vitality to the show, will be modified in such a fashion that:

(1) The House of Lords shall not be able to prevent the passage into law of measures concerted upon between the two Front Benches; and

(2) The House of Lords shall be able to prevent the passage of measures which, towards the end of a Parliament, are put up in order to secure the "swing of the pendulum."

In other words, so far as its powers are concerned, the Second Chamber will be turned into a machine subservient to the bi-party system.

Now as to its Constitution: The House of Lords is at present composed of some hundreds of men, the mass of whom owe their seats to heredity. A smaller number owe their seats to the filling of posts within the gift of the professional politicians, such as Colonial Governorships, etc. Another batch owe their seats to purchase–this base method is increasingly common, and has become taken for granted in our modern social habits. A fourth (small) class consists in men promoted in order to permit the easy working of the Party game–they have been in the way or proved failures on one of the two Front Benches. A tiny fifth class, consisting of less than half a dozen, are men who appear simply because they have rendered great services to their country; in one case a man of letters received this distinction. The lawyers, who must be present in small numbers in order to preserve the fiction of the House of Lords as a Court of Appeal, are a class apart. Then there are the Bishops.

Now, when the House of Lords is reconstituted, after due consultation and agreement between the two Front Benches, which of these classes will disappear? Not the handful of professional politicians already present; certainly not the peers who sit by right of purchase, for the sale of peerages is one of the most important aliments of the machine: still less the Bishops. Those who will disappear are the country squires who are in one sense really representative of England, and who, though usually bamboozled to some extent by the intrigues at Westminster, vote either in their own private interests or as they think best for the nation. Those are the men who will go. If new elements are added they will absolutely certainly include nominees of the machine, or, as the pretty phrase goes, "of the Crown."

Here is a concrete instance, and it will be well worth the while of any reader of this book to watch whether it has not been well chosen and whether its fulfilment does not prove to what a pass the political system has come.

It is necessary, then, for the understanding of modern British politics to realise that the two Front Benches are not two but one. They are united not only by the close bonds of relationship, intermarriage, and personal friendship which exist between them, but also by a common interest. It is to the interest of both to keep the game going, and it is also to the interest of both to prevent the game from becoming too real. It is, of course, quite true that, within these limits, each side genuinely wants to win. Apart from the sporting interest of the conflict, there are very material prizes to be gained by the winning side. To many politicians it makes a considerable pecuniary difference whether they are in office or in opposition—a fact which has decided many a political crisis, though we are all too well-bred to take it into our calculations. This, however, remains a secondary object, subordinate to the essential aim of both Front Benches, the maintenance of the Party System.

With the two Front Benches must be reckoned the Speaker and the Chairman of Committees, officers chosen by them, and working with them. It is no derogation of the admitted impartiality of the Chair to say this. There has never been the smallest reason to suspect the Speaker or Chairman of leaning unfairly to one or other side of the House. Why, indeed, should he, seeing that he at any rate knows the fight between them to be a sham one?

But it is well known that they continually consult with the leaders of the House and the Opposition as to the conduct of business, and that when the Front Benches are agreed they can almost invariably rely upon the support of the Chair.

Now, this governing group, as we may call it, comprising the two Front Benches and the Speaker, has attained absolute control over the procedure of the House of Commons.

First, it has the allotment of the time of the House. It can settle how much time shall be given to the discussion of any subject, and whether any time shall be given thereto. It can therefore in effect settle whether any particular measure shall have a chance of passing into law.

Secondly, it has control of the order of the House. It can settle what subjects may be discussed, and what may be said on those subjects.

To the consideration of these matters we shall now proceed.

# III

# THE HOUSE OF COMMONS AS IT IS

## The Control of the Time-Table

FTEN EMBEDDED in the stiff and unreal ritual of our Parliamentary system you will find some fragment which seems peculiarly fantastic and unmeaning, because it is really, so to speak, the fossil of a forgotten reality. One such case is the rule which compels persons accepting office to submit themselves to their constituents for re-election—a rule dating from the time when the House of Commons was supposed to be returned not to "support" the Government, but to oppose and criticise the Government. Another is the form gone through at every opening of Parliament of giving a first reading to a dummy bill before the King's Speech is delivered.

The object of this curious ceremony is to affirm the ancient privilege of the Commons to transact whatever business they chose without reference to the wishes of the Crown or its Ministers. It dates from the time when the Crown and the House were at war, and it emphasises the doctrine that the House can consider any subjects it likes, and consider them in any order it likes, is not bound to deal first with the matters brought before it by the Ministers. In other words, it affirms the absolute control of the House over its own time.

The symbol is still visible, but, alas! the fact it represented is gone. The House no longer controls its own time; the House no longer chooses its own subjects for discussion. These things are now done for it by the Ministers of the Crown.

Five-sixths or more of the time of the House is, under the present Standing Orders, at the absolute disposal of the Government.

It is devoted to the discussion of Bills proposed by the Ministers, or to the voting of supplies demanded by the Ministers. A certain amount of time is assigned by the Ministers to each matter, and at the end of that time the closure automatically puts an end to discussion. It is true that it is a part of the game for the Opposition to protest against such procedure, but the protest is merely ceremonial; for when a change takes place, the new Government invariably forgets its past utterances and uses the precedent set by its predecessor to restrict even more closely the rights of private members. Indeed, the farce of the Opposition protest has begun to pall even on politicians, and Mr Balfour has shown a disposition to drop it.

The private member has two and only two opportunities (apart from Supply, which we shall discuss later) of bringing any question in which he or his constituents may be specially interested before the House. In the ordinary way one afternoon a week is set aside for the discussion of business not brought forward by the two Front Benches. Even this privilege is held on a very insecure tenure. The Government can at any time demand all the time which this nominally representative and legislative assembly can give, and towards the end of a busy session it usually does so; but during the early part of the session a private member who is fortunate enough to secure a day may bring any question he likes before the House. The order of precedence for such questions is settled by balloting among the members.

The mode of bringing forward such a question may take the form either of a Bill or a resolution, but no opposed Bill has the smallest chance of passing into law unless the Ministers are prepared to grant special facilities. If this is not the case, the Bill, even if it passes its second reading by a large majority, is indefinitely shelved. We do not believe that there has been within recent years a single case of a private member's Bill, to which any opposition was offered, passing into law without special facilities from the Government. There have been innumerable cases of such Bills passed by large majorities in successive sessions, and even in successive Parliaments, yet never getting any further.

If the member confines himself to a resolution, desiring only to test the opinion of the House, it is by no means certain that he will be able to do so. It rests entirely with the Speaker to decide whether he will accept the closure at the end of the debate, so that a division may be taken before the House automatically adjourns, and very frequently he refuses to do so.

Moreover, it is nearly always possible for the Government to prevent a division on an inconvenient resolution by putting up one of its henchmen to move a shelving amendment. No better example of this could be chosen, nor any better test of the breakdown of representative institutions, as we now have them, than the lack of all machinery for the bringing forward of public questions. This is sufficiently proved when we say that so contemptuous a method as the above must under the present procedure of the House, be necessarily successful. A good illustration of this method was afforded when one of the authors of this book raised the question of the secrecy of the Party Funds. A "Liberal" barrister, Mr Buckmaster, was approached by the officials of the Executive, after full consultation with the Opposition Front Bench, asking whether he would undertake to nullify the debate. The matter was a ticklish one; when the motion was first tabled, many "experts in procedure" gravely hinted that it would be "out of order"—and it should be noted that whether a motion is declared out of order or not may not be known until the very moment before it is supposed to come on for discussion. Other hints were dropped as to the "pressure"—that is the promise of advantage or the refusal of advantage—that would be brought to bear; that is, that would be offered or threatened. The task of nullifying the debate was refused by more than one man; but at last the legal gentleman in question, presumably under some definite arrangement agreeable to himself, tabled an amendment to the effect that this secrecy was particularly bad in the case of the Tariff Reform League. This, of course, successfully put a stop to the discussion. The Unionists moved a similar amendment referring to the Free Trade Union; and the division, instead of being upon the secrecy of the Party Funds, was an ordinary party division between Liberals and Tories.

It is satisfactory to know that the reprisal threatened by one strong Radical among the many who desired the original discussion, to wit, going down to Cambridge and fighting Mr Buckmaster at the next election, was unnecessary. Mr Buckmaster lost his seat, and the two Front Benches were no doubt relieved to discover that they had thus escaped from their bargain.

Another expedient for preventing the raising of inconvenient questions by men acting in the interests of their constituents is the "blocking motion."

There is an absurd rule by which, if a member has given notice of a motion dealing with a certain question, no other member can discuss that question till the first member's motion is disposed of. As there is no obligation on the first member to move his motion, the Government finds it easy to burke discussion whenever it has a mind to do so. It has only to induce some obedient supporter to give notice of a motion that he has not the faintest intention of moving, and by keeping that motion indefinitely on the notice paper it can successfully prevent any other member from raising the question it desires to evade. In this way Mr Rees, now a knight or baronet in some order or other, distinguished himself during the Parliament of 1906. The most conspicuous example of an order proceeding from the two Front Benches to prevent discussion, by means of this fraudulent artifice in the hands of a subservient placeman, was the blocking of discussion on India, a matter of the most active and grave concern to everyone in these islands.

The method of raising questions by a motion for the adjournment of the House is hedged round with restrictions. It can only be done in the case of "a matter of urgent public importance," and the Speaker is the sole judge of what constitutes such a matter. The position and reputation of the Chair depend in this matter, perhaps more than in any other, upon a technical impartiality, and it should be recognised that in no matter is this impartiality more really or constantly exercised. The adjournment of the House is a grave matter interfering with the convenience and desires of many; it is exceedingly important to prevent its being frivolously moved. It may justly be said that if the matter really is of urgent public importance, the Chair still allows it to be an excuse for moving the adjournment. But—and this is essential—the mover must find forty members to support him, and if the Front Benches are united in desiring to prevent discussion, this is generally very difficult; for outside the Irish Party, which will probably have no concern in the matter, it is not easy to find forty members present in the House at one time (the House of Commons is usually attended by a dozen or twenty members at the most) who can afford to sacrifice the advantages in honour and money which the two Front Benches have to offer.

The general truth, then, is that the time of the House has passed absolutely into the hands of the little group that governs. The House cannot discuss what questions it pleases, or pass what laws it pleases. It can only wait obediently for the questions raised by the Government, and vote blindly for the laws which the Government chooses to introduce.

The vital importance of this phrase, "the time of the House," may escape the general reader. It lies in the fact that the Government (or, as our ancestors would have called it, "the Crown") can not only automatically fix how the time of the House shall be used, but can also decide *how much time there shall be*. That is the vital point. It is as though at a company meeting the directors had the power not only of saying what might be and what might not be raised by shareholders, not only the power of apportioning the time in which discussion should take place on each point, but also the power of saying whether such and such a question or all questions should be debated in meetings of so many hours' duration, and of fixing the number of meetings. Thus foreign affairs are not discussed at all in the English Parliament; a few hours a year are perfunctorily allotted to them; and the same is true of all those departments in which it is desired to avoid discussion. If the process continues we shall have in a few years no matter of vital and real interest open to discussion at a sufficient length for public opinion to be expressed, or for criticism to be allowed any weight.

There remains only a third method besides motions and bills, and that is the direct asking of a "question" in "question time." No speech is permitted, of course, on such an occasion, nor any characterisation of Ministerial action (though the Minister may make a speech in reply, and say what he likes about the questioner): nothing but a bare answer can be expected, and even that may be refused. But, such as it is, this method of keeping a subject alive by questions is the only–though paltry–procedure left to a member of the House of Commons who desires to act in that assembly in any representative character.*

With its efficiency and action we will deal in the next section.

## How It Works

That feature which the general public has least acquaintance with in political life is also the feature with which it should most concern itself: the machinery whereby representative action is nullified.

But, first of all, it is important to point out that this machinery is not a cause of the decline of Parliament; it is only a limiting condition of that decline. In other words, the machinery whereby all representative action of consequence is repressed is not a machinery continually applied nor acting regularly upon an organised body of resistance. Indeed, it would be better if this were so, for then its daily practice, the friction arising from it, and the public discussion which would necessarily follow, might weaken this particular section of the pathological conditions we are examining. This province of the disease might stand some chance of remedy.

The machinery which is here described is therefore most infrequent in its action, and not of a sort which can catch the public eye either by its outstanding character or by the frequency of its action. It applies only to rare and exceptional revolts against resistance.

In order to explain how this machinery applies, let us imagine some strong popular demand corresponding to the overwhelming popular demand for the immediate abolition of Chinese labour in the South African mines.

In the case of that popular demand we all know what happened. The country not only by an overwhelming majority, but with an

---

* Thus questions were the only opportunity Mr Wedgwood and others had of exposing the farce of the "Conference" of last summer. They were not ineffective.

overwhelming intensity, gave the mandate that the Chinese should go, and that they should go at once. It was a mandate based upon a mixture of popular emotions, not the least of which was the desire to chastise those South African Jews who had compelled our politicians as their servants to exploit for financial ends the popular enthusiasm in the matter of the South African war. It was, again, a demand for the signal punishment of the first attempt made since modern industrialism began, to move labour in large batches from place to place upon a scheme arranged by capital for the interests of capital alone. Popular instinct seized at once upon the enormous danger of that initial experiment, and perceived with sound sense that if it were not made an example of, and if the South African Jews were not taught a sharp lesson, the whole outlook and theory upon which this vile experiment had been based would become the permanent theory and outlook of international capitalism.

There were other features in the demand, some ignorant and some unwise, but the demand and the mandate were undeniably there.

The politicians, when the Parliament of 1906 had met, paid no attention whatsoever to the mandate. The leaders of the two Front Benches consulted with the South African Jews as to what would best suit their convenience. The South African Jews decided that they would be poorer men unless the Chinese were left to work out their contract, and especially insisted that the fresh batches of Chinese whom they had already ordered through the agency of the last Government should be supplied to them. They were indifferent to what should happen after the contracts slowly expired, for by that time local labour would be plentiful again, and cheap—at the end of the full four years probably cheaper than the continuation of the employment of the Chinese.

Such were the orders of these gentlemen, and the politicians had nothing to do but to obey. But how was it that, with the House of Commons crammed with men who had received a definite mandate from the electors to do the exact opposite to this, nothing was done to satisfy that mandate?

Some millions of the electors must have been asking themselves that question in their bewilderment at the action of Parliament immediately after the election; and of those millions a few hundreds at the most can have known how the thing was worked, so secret and so cunning are the workings by which the senile and fraudulent system proceeds.

Let us suppose a few years hence (for the populace are just now too weary of the politicians to initiate any democratic movement) a similar definite mandate upon some one subject.

For instance, let us suppose that the Duke of Battersea, a money dealer of sorts, born Heaven knows where, starts in the future some big development scheme involving the control over many thousands of labourers, the compulsory purchase of much land, and in general so large a public action as makes him need for its achievement the right to make by-laws and to enforce them under penalty, the right to segregate and to punish labourers, and the right to maintain a special police.

The hypothesis is not extravagant when you consider the pace at which industrialism is developing in this country, and the way in which the House of Commons has become the mere servant of the wealthy.

It is quite conceivable that the working classes would have brains and courage enough to revolt; there might be some such movement as there was over Chinese labour: a true popular initiative and mandate. It is quite certain that if any such symptoms of freedom showed themselves the Government Bench and the "Official Opposition" would combine, as they did over Chinese Labour, to repel the popular demand.

It is equally certain that they would succeed. The electorate feel that in their bones now, and that is what makes them indifferent to the whole dirty business.

But how, precisely, would the bosses succeed? What is the machinery which works the trick? It cannot be too often repeated that the prime cause of the whole matter is the profound corruption of the Parliamentary system. Batches of lawyers expecting money rewards from the two Front Benches, not one of whom would dream of acting as a representative: batches of elderly wealthy men waiting for honours from the two Front Benches, not one of whom would be such a fool as to lose the honour by representative action: groups of wealthy men who by the aid they afford to others, by the fear their economic power inspires, by their control over the Press by advertisements or direct ownership, are more powerful over their Parliamentary dependants than the officers of an army over their commands, and who know that representative action would lose them their Government contracts and their lucrative opportunities in the un-free dependencies of the Crown: some fifty or sixty or more, each of whom regards himself as a candidate for the reception of public money in the form of a salary, and that salary only to be obtained by abstaining from any representative action and obeying the two Front Benches: the Secretaries of Ministers and of ex-Ministers; the thirty or forty occupants of the Front Benches themselves—all these between them make up (when we have excepted the Irish Party, which is happily independent of such intrigue[16]) the great bulk of Parliament.

But among those hundreds some few would probably be found—perhaps as many as half a dozen—who by temperament or even by self-interest and calculation would be moved to express the demand of the many millions who had constituted the new Parliament. Some one or two, in other words, will attempt to act in a representative fashion. It is then that the machinery would begin to work, and that machinery we will now proceed to explain.

The new Parliament has met; the first few days, in which the memory of the election is still strong upon members, are not yet expired. The earliest opportunity for action occurs in the debate on the Address. After the Speech from the Throne has been delivered, the House of Commons debates for a few days upon the reply to that Address. And any dissatisfaction at the action or inaction of the Government, as expressed in the King's Speech, must take the form of an amendment regretting that such and such a policy has not been mentioned in that Speech, or has been mentioned in it.

Mr Brown and Mr Jenks note the absence in the King's Speech of any mention of the Government's intention to cancel the policy of the last Government with regard to the great Land Development Company formed by the Duke of Battersea, with its proposed obnoxious by-laws, special police, and other features odious to the populace. On this point the elections turned, and, like Chinese labour, the elections turned on it by a spontaneous effort of the populace, in spite of the vigorous, not to say frenzied, efforts of the bosses; among whom must be included of course not only the leaders of the two Front Benches, but the whole vast machine which, by secret funds, innumerable paid agents, local and central, etc., "runs" a General Election.

Well, Mr Brown and Mr Jenks put down an amendment on the paper, humbly regretting that His Gracious Majesty (who is by a Constitutional fiction the author of his own speech) has not promised to cancel the Duke of Battersea's little job.

Nothing can prevent these gentlemen putting down the said amendment. So wide are our liberties that unless the phrases chosen contain expressions which the officials of the House (who are part of the machine) consider offensive or intemperate or frivolous, nothing could prevent Mr Brown and Mr Jenks from putting that amendment down.

Now, the curious reader will note that nothing prevents anyone of the remaining six hundred men from putting down amendments, or, to speak more accurately, nothing prevents the so-called "Opposition" half from doing so; for it is part of the game that an "Opposition" man putting down an amendment to a Government policy will not spoil his future chance of a salary, contract, baronetcy or what not, on condition that he puts nothing down which has not been allowed by secret understanding between the two Front Benches. When, therefore, it is heard that Mr Brown and Mr Jenks, manfully sacrificing all hope of baronetcies, contracts, or salaries, have put down their highly representative amendment, a dozen or twenty amendments will appear on the paper dealing with as many different subjects, many of which probably were not and could not be in the mind of any of the electorate at the time of the election. Any subject will do so long as it serves to swell the list.

Therefore, even if discussion were not limited, and if the rules of the House allowed discussion to be free, Mr Brown and Mr

Jenks' amendment might come very late in the list, and some other hare might have been started to entertain the public, so that their action should fall flat.

But these "even ifs" do not apply.

In the first place there is your "Official Opposition Amendment." You may protest that the Constitution and the very theory of self-government can know nothing of an "Official Opposition"; that the phrase in connection with self-government or representation is ridiculous; but it is the chief reality of the machine and the most notable wheel in the empty grinding of Parliament. The Official Opposition Amendment must be taken first. It is, of course, upon some subject agreed upon between the bosses, and not within a hundred miles of the popular mandate which Mr Brown and Mr Jenks have attempted to express.

What of the other amendments? Are they taken by lot or in the order of time in which they were set down? By no means. They are taken in the order in which the Chair decides, and the Chair is of course one with the two Front Benches in such matters. I mean where the matter is of real and sufficient gravity. For here, as elsewhere throughout this book, it must be protested that among the wheels of the machine that which is least open to criticism, and among the decayed functions of Parliament that which preserves the old and free conditions most, is the Chair. Subject to the rules and traditions which so greatly favour the bosses and their nominees, the action of the Chair is singularly impartial; but when something really grave—like Chinese Labour, for instance—which the two Front Benches had determined to settle in a manner of their own is on the carpet, the Chair cannot be impartial, for to be impartial would be to take the side of the people against the politicians, and it is no part of Mr Speaker's duty to consider the people. He is there to give, subject to the rules and customs of Parliament, a fair and equal chance to every member, and no more, to preserve the courtesies of debate, to keep speakers to the point, and so forth. If he were to give Mr Brown and Mr Jenks priority over, say, Mr Isaacs' amendment about the Seychelles Islands, he would be giving preference to two men as against forty or fifty who have assured him that Mr Isaacs' amendment is what they really care about. It is quite certain, therefore, that Mr Brown and Mr Jenks will come very far down the list, perhaps at the end of it.

Even so, by patiently waiting, their turn will come; and if the electorate is not by that time sick and tired of the whole wretched humbug, they could, by moving that amendment, put the bosses into a very pretty hole: for those who vote against the amendment would be flying in face of their election promises so very soon after the election, and while opinion was still so hot, that they might jeopardise their seats, and with their seats the prospective baronetcies, salaries, and contracts aforesaid.

But wait a moment. The turn of Mr Brown and Mr Jenks will never come. The bosses have not only the power of raising sham discussion, they have not only the power of extending to any number those sham discussions, they have also the power over Time; it is the leaders of the two Front Benches who decide in consultation among themselves, and after discovering from their local agents and central agents whether the popular temper is getting dangerous upon the subject, how long the debate on the Address will last. They certainly will not let it last long enough for Mr Brown and Mr Jenks to enjoy their little show. Those valiant men have sacrificed the "prizes" of the game and all their chance of boodle for nothing at all.

What further action can they take?

As we have seen in the former section, by the theory and practice of Parliament three opportunities, and three alone, are open to these worthy men in their quixotic desire to represent their constituents:

(a) Any member of Parliament may bring in a Bill; he may do so under what is called the Ten Minutes Rule, or he may do so in a more thorough manner if he happens to have the luck of the ballot.

Members ballot for the right to bring in so many Bills; and each individual member's chance may be ascertained by dividing the number 670 [the number of members of the British Parliament. —Ed.] by the number of days which the party bosses allow for this amiable and harmless entertainment. Sometimes they will allow as much as, say, twenty-five days; then Jenks and Brown may count on having about one chance in twelve between them; but if they only allow a dozen days, then Jenks and Brown only have one chance in twenty-four.

Let not the reader imagine that bringing in a Bill is the simple thing that laymen would take it to be. The Bill may be out of order; it may be supposed to cover the ground of what the Government have already decided to do, or it may contravene any one of those obscure and almost innumerable rules which not half a dozen experts have mastered in the last thirty years. A Bill brought in under the Ten Minutes Rule is of course an absurdity from the point of view of getting anything done. Bills are thus brought in only to give public notice of the grievance they are to remedy, or the right it is hoped to confer. But a Bill brought in through the luck of the ballot has the advantage of a whole afternoon's debate.

What then?

Well, after that there is nothing, unless the two Front Benches agree to allow further stages; the bringing in of a Bill simply means an afternoon wasted in academic debate. A Bill becomes an Act of Parliament only after it has been read a first time, read a second time, debated in its general principles, then sat upon by a Committee, special or general; then in its amended stage read a third time, then passed by the House of Lords and assented to by the Crown. The two Front Benches, having control of the time of the House of Commons, always see to it that no Bill which does not suit their convenience shall proceed beyond the first formal stage. And none ever does. When you read in your paper of how the Hon. Charles Lake cleverly piloted the Washerwomen's Bill through Committee, and after years of struggle made it law, "though it was but a private member's Bill," you are reading one of those conventional falsehoods which are used to deceive the public. There is no such thing as piloting a Bill. What you do, if you have a private Bill to which the bosses cannot object (as we may conceive the Hon. Charles Lake's Bill to have been), is to put pressure by means of lady friends or your newspaper, or in some other way, upon the bosses, so that when they can allow time in a slack moment the whole of the stages shall be gone through. The Bills that pass in this way have never any real significance.

We need hardly say that Jenks and Brown's Bill to prevent the Government backing up the Duke of Battersea's concession, even if they had the luck of the ballot, would never go to Committee.

But would it be divided upon?

It might or might not be divided upon, according as the two Front Benches chose. It might be decided that the matter was of such importance that a bare afternoon's discussion was not enough for a division to be allowed upon it. Or again, an amendment might be accepted and debated in its place; at any rate the poor off-chance of bringing in a Bill is useless.

(b) A member with a similar luck in the ballot may use his day to bring in a motion.

A motion, of course, is of no legal effect whatsoever. It is mere hot air. It has the one advantage of provoking a division, but here again that division will or will not take place, precisely as the Front Benches may decide.*

Upon Brown and Jenks' motion, if they have the luck of the ballot (say one in twelve or one in twenty or one in thirty), and bring it in, no division will be taken: the Front Benches will see to that.

Of course, it need hardly be pointed out that Brown and Jenks bringing in a motion or a Bill to this effect could only be done if it were done with the utmost secrecy. If the two Front Benches got wind of it, nay, if any but a few of their hundreds of supporters got wind of it, the bosses would arrange with some hack who was waiting for a salary or a title to put down a fictitious motion upon the paper. Once a man has a motion down, no similar motion can be debated; but, by a rule invented for the purpose of carrying on the machine, a motion may be kept on the paper, although the mover refuses to have it debated. The hack, therefore, will put down a motion, covering the point which Brown and Jenks are

---

* When one of the joint authors of this book brought in his motion for the auditing of the secret Party Funds, the Front Benches put up an amendment which turned the debate into a discussion upon the abstract economic merits of Free Trade, and to this day no one knows the opinion of any member of the House of Commons, as expressed by vote, upon this most corrupt feature of all the corrupt features of Parliamentary life.

going to raise, leave it indefinitely on the paper, refuse to have it debated, and so prevent its arising in the House at all. Thus a liberal manufacturer may solemnly put down a motion to discuss the sale of peerages; a Jew may put down a motion to discuss the abuse of money-lending; a High Churchman a motion to discuss the practices of the High Church; a Catholic a motion to provide for the inspection of convents, and so forth. The action is, by the custom of Parliament, taken in the Pickwickian sense.

(c) Brown and Jenks may ask questions.

Such a point has the degradation of Parliament reached that this shred of the old representative power is truly, literally, and without exaggeration, the only active part of that power now remaining. Small and inept as it would seem among a democratic people and in a free assembly, it is today, in comparison with the rest that goes on in Parliament, of capital importance.

The Chair rules that no Minister is bound to answer a question. How old this ruling may be is not to the point; it would in theory seem to limit the value of questioning so strictly as almost to destroy it. As a matter of fact, however, some sort of answer is usually attempted. Nineteen-twentieths of the questions asked concern administrative points on which the answer is not a Minister's, but that of a permanent official for whom the Minister speaks in the House.*

There is little doubt that this valuable, or comparatively valuable, privilege of questioning the Ministers will be curtailed in the near future, for it has already on several occasions given anxiety to the two Front Benches. But for the moment it is fairly free. Three whole quarters of an hour a day are allotted to questions, and a supplementary question may be asked, arising out of the original one.

True, Ministerial answers on a point as important as the Duke of Battersea's concession would be valueless; they would be ambiguous, general, humorous, or quite off the point. But questions habitually asked by Brown and Jenks would at least suffice to keep the matter alive, and possibly some particularly nasty side of the

---

* This is notably the case with Foreign Office questions, as has been conspicuously apparent in the last two Parliaments, where the Foreign Minister had no personal knowledge of foreign affairs, nor of the languages, places, peoples etc., involved in them.

scandal, which could not otherwise be ventilated, might be made public in this fashion.*

But though questions are thus valuable as advertisement, they are quite useless as a means of action. The Ayrshire Foundry scandal, for instance, to which allusion has just been made in a note, was exposed by means of questions to the House of Commons, but it was kept from the public, who are still in the main ignorant of it, and no action whatever followed upon the exposure. No one was punished, and the same thing might happen again tomorrow, without any consequences of unpleasantness to the culprits.

With these three methods–bills, motions, and questions–the power of Brown and Jenks is exhausted. We have seen that as methods of action all three are useless. In other words, no representative action on the chief matter of a general election, if that matter has proceeded from the electors and does not suit the private interests of the professional politicians, can take place; and, so far as the representative power of members is concerned, the House of Commons is dead.

There can be all the sham fight you will upon the sham issues which the bosses have arranged between themselves before an election takes place, but there can be no initiative on the part of the electorate which shall have any chance of acting upon the assembly at Westminster.

## A Concrete Example

In order to give the reader a clear idea of this monstrosity (for it is no less), let him consider the following case: Public circumstances have rendered it acutely necessary to pay certain sums of public money to a large class of individuals upon a certain date, if widespread misery is to be avoided.

There is a conflict upon the area of distress which this vote of public money is to cover. Some say that the famine or what not is only acute in Lancashire south of the Ribble; but those who

---

* Thus the Ayrshire Foundry scandal, in which Campbell-Bannerman was mixed up, was exposed by means of questions.

know most about the local circumstances are confident that the West Riding, though less hard hit than South Lancashire, is still in acute necessity of relief.

A Bill is drafted and introduced by the Chancellor of the Exchequer, in the first clause of which it is provided that on a certain date he shall be authorised to pay such and such sums to authorities or individuals appearing later in the Bill. The exact words run:

> On or not later than the first of August 1910, every person hereinafter named, and the authorities hereinafter named, shall be entitled to receive....

and after that follow the amounts proposed.

Several clauses are necessary, twenty perhaps, to make the Bill workable in view of the various circumstances, previous laws, and local arrangements affected by it. Let us suppose that the fifteenth clause is that which, in effect, confines the action of the Bill to South Lancashire.

Here we are dealing with an exceptionally favourable case, for we suppose no opposition from those relatives and friends of Ministers who happen to sit on the other Front Bench; such a Bill would be "non-controversial."

But a number of amendments are suggested, for though the principle of the Bill is accepted by nearly everybody, yet many changes in its provisions would make it more acceptable to this or that interest in the House. The amendments are put down; advantage is, of course, taken of the position by those few who oppose the Bill altogether. The first amendment in order is one thus framed:

> Distress Relief Bill: Clause I, Line 6.–Leave out from the word 'every' to the word 'receive,' and substitute the words 'to every person hereinafter named there shall be paid' for the words so deleted.

Many other amendments are on the paper, but this is the first of them, because it applies to the earliest words in the Bill that can be amended at all.* On Clause XV., however, the really vital

---

* The very first words of every Bill are a standing formula, "Be it enacted by the King's Most Excellent Majesty, etc., etc."

amendment affecting some millions of human beings, of immense importance in the eyes of many members of the House, set down by them in several forms, and of no less effect than to include the whole of the West Riding in the measure, is to be debated. It is known that the Treasury, from motives of economy, desires to limit—as indeed its Bill sets forth—the relief to South Lancashire alone.

Now, then. This is what we will suppose to happen in Committee.

The amendment suggesting that "to every person shall be *paid*," instead of "every person shall be entitled to *receive*," comes on first.

The Chairman of Committees is in the Chair. He calls upon the mover of the amendment, or selects one name out of several if the amendment has been put down by several people. The mover rises and makes a speech, of not quite a page of Hansard* in length; at the end of that speech the amendment is proposed to the House. The Chancellor of the Exchequer makes a short speech in reply, saying that he does not see that the amendment is of much value; the mover gets up and answers this short speech in another short speech, apologising for the amendment, and showing why he put it down. The Chancellor of the Exchequer gets up again, and makes a rather longer speech, reasserting his opinion that the amendment is of no great value. After the Chancellor another Front Bench man gets up and makes a speech in which he says that the "Official Opposition" will not support the amendment (sighs of relief on the part of those who would have had to vote for the tomfoolery if the Official Opposition *had* supported it). When the Front Bench man has sat down, another gentleman gets up and makes a rather longer speech in support of the amendment; he is followed by a fifth speaker, who makes the longest speech of all. Altogether, four pages of Hansard are taken up on this absolutely futile point, there is a division, and the absurd amendment is of course lost.

---

* Hansard's Reports—now succeeded by the Official Reports—are (or were) the fullest available reports of speeches. Those of all save men of Cabinet rank are somewhat condensed, but they are sufficiently accurate to afford the most practical standard of measurement, both of time and of number, of words occupied in a debate. The pages are close printed and in double column.

Two more amendments, affecting the words immediately following in the Bill, are duly debated, and each duly withdrawn without division. A fourth amendment (coming within two lines of the first in this lengthy Bill) is to the effect that the law shall be law "until Parliament otherwise determines"—in other words, the law shall be law until Parliament chooses to repeal it. Considering that Parliament has the right to make and repeal laws at pleasure, the plain man would imagine such an amendment to be out of order. Nothing of the kind. It is made the starting-point of a perfectly enormous debate! The mover speaks for more than a page of Hansard; the Chancellor of the Exchequer replies in another page; a member of the so-called "Opposition" Front Bench talks half a page; three private members then consume a page and a half. Another member of the so-called "Opposition" Bench talks another page; yet another page is occupied by half a dozen private members who take up a great deal of the time of the House, but who are somewhat condensed in the official report. Then up gets the "leader" of the "Opposition," and talks for a mortal page and a half on this absurdity; he is followed by the Prime Minister for half a page; two more "Opposition" Front Bench men and two private members account for another page. And this ridiculous palaver is not concluded until nearly nine pages of Hansard's Reports are exhausted! There is a division, and (of course) the meaningless amendment is lost.

Immediately after, in the very next line, it is proposed to leave out the words "under this Act." In other words, it is proposed to make a verbal alteration which negatives the Bill. That also is in order! It is duly debated, and then great heavens!—withdrawn! In the same line yet *another* amendment proposes that the law shall only work so long as its conditions are fulfilled; that is, that the law shall only be operative so long as it can legally be operative.... And that is in order! And *that* is duly debated! And *that* in its turn, to the bewilderment of some unsophisticated member of the public watching from the gallery, is withdrawn!

In the very next line (and the Bill has perhaps 150 lines)....But we will not detain the reader further. Let it suffice to say that when the whole day has been exhausted, Parliament has advanced in this sort of debate through exactly seven lines of the Bill, and in that advance has changed absolutely nothing!

Day follows day; amendments of this sort pour in one on top of the other, and at last, when perhaps a tithe in mere space of the Bill has been thus "debated," and long before the vital amendment on Clause XV. has been reached, the two Front Benches decide that the House must now turn to other business, the rest of the Bill is closured, and there is an end of it. The people of the West Riding are left without relief, and, so far as they are concerned, they need not have been at the pains of sending their members to Westminster at all; their views and necessities have not been so much as expressed.

The reader will be inclined to say that such inanity, however far the degradation of Parliament may have fallen, is impossible; that the picture here drawn is a caricature, and can make no pretence to be a true picture.

Well, for "South Lancashire" substitute destitute people of over seventy years of age; substitute for the "Distress Relief Bill" the Old Age Pensions Bill, and for "The West Riding" substitute "destitute old people between sixty-five and seventy," and you have an exact and literal account of what took place in the opening of the proceedings in Committee in the summer of 1908, when the Old Age Pensions Bill was being "piloted through the House"–to use the professional phrase consecrated to that futile performance. The supreme question, the one thing that most mattered to the destitute, was dealt with precisely as a despotic monarchy would deal with it, but without the moral right and position which lies behind a despotic monarchy; the procedure of the House had been used simply to cheat the people, and very effectively was that bit of cheating done.

## "The Tone of the House"

There pervades the House of Commons a certain moral atmosphere conventionally called "the Tone of the House."

All corporate bodies, a school, a regiment, a household, present this phenomenon, and the House of Commons is no exception to the rule.

"The Tone of the House" would of course be somewhat modified by a renewal of its *personnel;* it would be greatly modified by even a slight modification of its rules; it would not be the same were a different type of man chosen for its officers.

In the absence of any of these changes it continues, changing only slightly as men change, and the times.

It is the subject of deserved and widespread ridicule; men entering politics are warned by their experienced friends against suffering its influence. It is not a good moral atmosphere; it is a stupid and rather a degraded one, much lower than that of the House of Lords, for instance, and not to be compared with that of a good college or a good regiment. But for the purposes of this book our only concern is to ask how far it may be responsible for that disease whose last phase and disastrous effect we are here studying. How far is the Party System, with its two sham sets of opponents, its huge salaries and the rest, dependent upon "the Tone of the House"?

The answer of one who has had some years' experience of that atmosphere can only be that it is a far smaller factor in the Party System than those of the public who are palled by "the Tone of the House" when they come across it during their presence at occasional debates might imagine. "The Tone of the House" makes impossible any *stimulus* applied from within: and that is true, let it be remembered, of every traditional and corporate body. Such stimuli are, from the point of view of a corporate body's traditions, mere disorder, and are resented as such. But it does not render impossible decisive action; what renders that impossible, or rather very difficult, is the code of rules under which the House now debates; it is only very occasionally that some subject of definite national import can be brought up in the House of Commons, and a man must be either very lucky in the ballot or have some exceptional opportunity to compel the House of Commons to consider anything which the double machine does not want considered. But it is not "the Tone of the House" that prevents decisive action of this sort; these hundreds of men confined hour after hour in a dreary building, the physical air of which is unwholesome and domestic decoration appalling, are glad enough of any breeze, moral or material. It may verily be said that an anarchist attempt to blow the place up would, if the explosion were sufficiently distant, be welcomed as a break in the crass futility and monotony of the dull and wholly empty round. There is indeed only one way in which "the Tone of the House" prevents action, and therefore supports the hypocritical nonsense of the professionals, and that is, that it tends to capture any man whose motive is not wholeheartedly a motive of achievement. It is certainly an atmosphere in which it is much easier not to bother, and a man who partly wants reform, but partly also good fellowship, and a sense of ease in his surroundings, will find after a very few months that the proportion of his desire for reform to his other desires has sunk to zero. But "the Tone of the House" is purely negative, even here, and quite a few men sufficiently determined to destroy the Front Bench arrangements from within could do so; a dozen would be amply sufficient.*

No, "the Tone of the House" has never proved sufficiently strong to prevent, on the rare occasions when such a thing was possible, a damaging attack upon the machine; that is prevented in a manner much more direct, namely, by the grip, through secret Party Funds, the control of elections, and the choice of candidates in the constituencies, held upon Parliament by the machine. To these practical points the reader must pay a particular attention. They are the most important of all the concrete objects which reformers have before them to attack. With their method of corruption we will now deal.

---

* It has often been suggested by those unacquainted with Westminster that the breakdown of the Labour Party and its absorption and digestion by the professional politicians was due to this influence of "the Tone of the House." The suggestion is plausible, but inaccurate. "The Tone of the House" certainly made the good speakers in the party much worse speakers than they might have become—for "the Tone of the House" is death to rhetoric; but the definite capitulation of the Labour men to the two Front Benches and the disappearance of the Labour Party as an active force was due to something far less subtle than any "Tone." It was due to a definite compact with the Executive by which places, advantage in moving motions, etc.—ultimately, perhaps, Cabinet rank—should be the price of compromise: the bargain was accepted.

# IV

# THE SECRET FUNDS

### The Unmentionable Truth

T IS CHARACTERISTIC that the most important fact about English politics is the fact that nobody mentions. The two party organisations of which we have spoken are supported by means of two huge war-chests. Money is urgently needed at every point in the modern political game; and money is found.

Whence does that money come? Whither does it go? These are questions which cannot be answered with any certainty; it is our whole case that they cannot be so answered. The Party Funds are secretly subscribed; they are secretly disbursed. No light is thrown upon their collection save that which the annual Honours List furnishes. No light is thrown upon their expenditure save that which the division list may supply. But, briefly, it may be said that they are subscribed by rich men who want some advantage, financial or social, from the Government, and that they are spent in paying the expenses of members of Parliament – in other words, in corrupting the legislature.

The total amount so raised and spent must necessarily be a matter of conjecture. But there is no doubt that it must be enormous. Anyone who has had the good fortune to fight an election with the party organisation at his back knows that he has only to ask and to have. It is part of the game for the party organisers to proclaim themselves to be in a state of perennial penury – to declare that the raising of the funds was a matter of immense difficulty, and to issue elaborate bogus appeals to "working men" and others to give their mites to the cause. As a matter of fact, there will never be any lack of funds for either party so long as each has its fair share of power and patronage and the supply of peerages and baronetcies is unchecked

The funds are expended exactly as the Secret Service Funds of Walpole were expended in buying votes. The affair is more delicately arranged than it was in Walpole's time. Instead of paying members of Parliament, *after* they are elected, to vote in accordance with the wishes of the Government, the governing gang take care that no one shall be elected a member of Parliament who is not prepared so to vote. This is certainly more decent, probably cheaper, and has the enormous advantage of eliminating the chance of an incorruptible member. In principle it is the same thing. The effect of paying a man's election expenses out of a secret fund at the disposal of the party organisers is that the member becomes responsible not to his constituents, but to the caucus which pays him. If he opposes some fad of the party organisers or their paymasters, however popular his attitude may be with the electors, the governing gang will find a way to get rid of him, either by the withdrawal of funds, by pressure on the local organisation, or, if all other methods fail, by running an official party candidate against him.

But what must especially be insisted on is this, that the very existence of this powerful engine for the corruption of Parliamentary representation is carefully kept secret from the mass of the people. Not one man in thirty knows that there are such things as Party funds; not one man in a hundred has the faintest idea of how they are raised and spent; not one man in a thousand realises that they are almost the most important factor in English politics. A deliberate reserve is observed on both sides concerning the whole subject. The politicians do not want it ventilated. They love darkness rather than light—for a reason mentioned in Scripture, but veiled impenetrably from the modern intellect.

## The Sale of Legislative Power

The ordinary method of replenishing the Party Funds is by the sale of peerages, baronetcies, knighthoods, and other honours in return for subscriptions. This traffic is notorious. Everyone acquainted in the smallest degree with the inside of politics knows that there is a market for peerages in Downing Street, as he knows that there is a market for cabbages in Covent Garden;[17] he could put his finger upon the very names of the men who have bought their "honours." Yet the ordinary man is either ignorant of the truth or only darkly suspects it. And most of those who know about it are afraid to bring the facts to light by quoting names and instances, because the administration of our law of libel weighs the scales of justice heavily in favour of the rich, and because a particular case could only be proved if one were able to do—what one would not perhaps be allowed to do—to subpoena the party managers and demand that the party accounts should be brought into court.

Perhaps the best way, on the whole, to bring home to the average man the real nature of the scandal is for him to glance through the Honours List for any year and ask himself why any of the people mentioned therein were honoured. The case of peerages is specially strong, because a peerage conveys not only dignity but legislative power. A Peer is a Senator. He is supposed to be a man called to the Council of the Nations because he is in some way especially fitted to advise on some matters of public policy. Now, among ten peers created during the last twenty years you could pick out some half-dozen answering passably to that description—Lords Peel, Kitchener, Curzon, Morley of Blackburn, Fisher, and a few more. Why were the rest made peers? On what conceivable ground is it claimed that their services are necessary to the Government of the Nation?

Take only the Birthday Honours List for the year 1910, framed by the advice of a "Liberal" Government in the act of denouncing "the Peers" in foolish and immoderate language. It includes seven peers. Coronets were bestowed on the Rt. Hon. R. K. Causton, Sir Walter Foster, Sir Hudson Kearley, Sir Weetman Pearson, Sir William Hay Holland, Mr Freeman-Thomas, and Sir Christopher Furness. Among the recipients of lesser honours are one of the "Liberal" scions of the great house of Harmsworth—a brother of Lord Northcliffe of the Isle of Thanet, whom a conservative Government lately thought worthy to be a member of the Senate, – Mr (now Sir Alfred) Mond of Brunner, Mond & Co., and a Mr Charles (or Carl) Mayer.

Now, considering only the peers, what are their qualifications? Remember that the qualification required is a qualification not merely for public honours, but for a seat in the Senate, and legislative power equal even in theory to that of some ten to thirty thousand ordinary men, and in practice, of course, indefinitely greater.

Sir Walter Foster (Lord Ilkeston) is of the seven the one of whom it could best be maintained that he deserved his peerage on public grounds. He is a distinguished medical man, and an eminent man of science. A fact which probably weighed more with those who ennobled him was that he had been President of the National Liberal Federation. But the true reason for his elevation was undoubtedly that he consented to give up a safe seat in the House of Commons in order to make room for Colonel Seely, one of the Front Benchers, whose own constituents had rejected him.

Mr Causton (now Lord Southwark) is a very wealthy man, who held during the years 1906 to 1910 the unpaid office of Paymaster of the Forces. He was rejected by the electors of Southwark in January 1910, and probably received his new honour as a sort of consolation prize and in recognition of his previous services to the Party. But, remember, it was much more than an honour. It was a right to make and unmake laws for England.

Sir Christopher Furness (now Lord Furness) is the head of a great engineering and shipbuilding firm, a very rich man, and a pillar of the Liberal Party. He was elected for West Hartlepool at the General Election of January 1910, but was unseated on petition for the errors and irregularities of his agents. He himself, of course, left the court without a stain on his character. He promptly received a coronet, and the right to make and unmake laws.

Sir William Holland (created Lord Rotherham) was an enormously rich cotton-owner of Lancashire. No reason can be assigned for giving him and his heirs in perpetuity the right to legislate except his great wealth and the use he probably made of it in support of his party.

Sir Hudson Kearley (now Lord Devonport) was the head of a very large firm of importers and merchants. He made a great deal of money in trade, and probably spent some of it in the service of his party. He also served gratuitously as Chairman of the Port of London Authority. Nothing else of importance is known of him; and the reasons for his elevation have not been divulged.

Mr Freeman Freeman-Thomas (now Lord Willingdon) was another wealthy and well-connected Liberal MP. He is the grandson of Lord Hampden, and the son-in-law of Lord Brassey. He was prominently associated with Lord Rosebery's ill-starred "Liberal League." Nothing but party services can be alleged as an excuse for ennobling him.

Sir Weetman Pearson is the head of a great contracting company, to which Mr Lloyd-George, junior, son of the Chancellor of the Exchequer, has recently been articled. He is a very rich man, and there is an end of it. He is now Lord Cowdray.

These examples are all taken from last year's Honours List of the present Liberal Government. But it must not be supposed that the examination of any Conservative Honours List would yield results in any way more respectable. In point of fact nothing is better calculated to show the essential unity of the two rings which run the "Liberal" and "Conservative" parties than a comparison of the way in which peerages are bestowed by both. The "Liberals" are perhaps the worst sinners in that they make democratic professions which are not made (or at any rate not made so strenuously) by their opponents. But this is really all the difference between them. Indeed, it often happens that rich families contribute to both party war-chests, and so get a double share of recognition.

The family of Guest, a wealthy family, with large estates in Dorsetshire, were for many years Conservatives, and their powerful territorial influence made them a tower of strength to Conservatism in that part of England. The head of the family, Ivor Guest, received the title of Lord Wimborne from his party in 1880. In 1904 the Guests passed over to the Liberal side, and the tactics by which they had brought the truths of Conservatism home to their tenants were now used to put before them with equal cogency an opposite view. The Hon. Ivor Guest, the eldest son of Lord Wimborne, was particularly active in promoting the political creed to which he had been so recently converted. He performed in its support the functions which bear in the Party System the technical name of "social." In no other respect was he other than a mediocrity. In the crisis of 1909, just when the politicians were loudest in their denunciation of the Peers, the Guest peerage was actually doubled, and the Hon. Ivor Guest became Lord Asby St Ledger. In his case it cannot even be pleaded, as some will perhaps plead in the cases of Sir Weetman Pearson or Sir William Holland, that he has served his country as an organiser of enterprise and industry. He never in his life did anything at all to merit special notice, nor ever will. Yet a Liberal Government thought him a proper recipient of that hereditary legislative power which they have pretended to hold in abhorrence.

A significant case may be noted in the same Honours List which we have just examined. Not very many years have passed since a Conservative Government moved the derision of the world by creating Mr Alfred Harmsworth first a baronet and then a peer, with the title of Lord Northcliffe of the Isle of Thanet. Lord Northcliffe has no children, so that it might be expected that with the death of its first possessor the title would also die. But it is evident that our rulers do not think fit that the memory of so remarkable an event as the enrolment of the proprietor of *Answers* among the barons of England should so soon perish. Though Lord Northcliffe has no sons, he has a large company of brothers, and it will be noted that one of these has been chosen by a Liberal Government for a baronetcy, and this will doubtless be for him, as it was for his brother, a stepping stone to full nobility. Sir Harold Harmsworth has not even the claims of Lord Northcliffe to distinction. Lord Northcliffe at least produced *Answers* and *The Daily Mail.* We are as yet unaware of anything good or bad that Sir Harold has produced. Nevertheless, the new peerage, which we may confidently expect in a year or so, should the Liberals remain in power, will at any rate serve to show that what the Conservative Party managers have planted, the Liberal Party managers are only too ready to water.

## The Sale of Policies

The sale of honours, including the sale of legislative power, is the ordinary method by which the Party Funds are replenished, but it is by no means the most socially mischievous method. Side by side with the traffic in honours there is a much more insidious traffic in policies. Many rich men subscribe secretly to the Party Funds in order to get a "pull" or a measure of control over the machine which governs the country—sometimes to promote some private fad of their own, but more often simply to promote their commercial interests.

It is notorious that the late Mr Cecil Rhodes[18] did this on a large scale. Letters have been published which passed between him and the late Mr Shnadhorst,[19] then head of the Liberal Caucus. Mr Rhodes, than whom none knew men and methods better, offers sums running into tens of thousands to the Liberal Party Funds, but makes it a condition that Egypt shall remain under British government, and that a Liberal Ministry shall look with favourable eyes on his scheme for a Cape to Cairo railway. It does not appear that he ever received in writing any definite promise, but Mr Schnadhorst appears to have satisfied him. Anyhow, it is not denied (a) that the money was paid, and (b) that the Liberal Government did not evacuate Egypt, though Mr Gladstone, who was supposed to lead the Liberal Party, had publicly declared himself in favour of evacuation. We have nothing to say here about the desirability or undesirability of evacuating Egypt. That the evacuation of Egypt would have been disastrous we are not concerned to dispute. But the solution of this question ought to be settled by statesmen on grounds of statesmanship, and not dictated by a single rich subscriber to the Party Funds. For if a policy of which we may approve can be obtained by purchase, its negative is open to a higher bidder. As it was, Gladstone, though nominally leader, was at the mercy of Schnadhorst, and Schnadhorst was at the mercy of anyone who would give him money.

Things have undoubtedly got worse since these events took place, but the impenetrable darkness in which all such transactions are veiled makes it increasingly difficult to give specific instances.

There has occurred, however, another interesting case within the last ten years, a case which primarily concerns the other political party.

In 1903 Dr Rutherfoord Harris, the well-known South African financier, was contesting Dulwich at a bye-election in the Conservative interest. Being used to the franker methods of young and vigorous communities, he announced publicly that he had sent £10,000 to the Conservative Party Funds. The candour of this announcement somewhat perturbed for a moment the placidity of British politics. But the commentary was yet to come. It came when a month or so afterwards a Conservative Government, acting against the best traditions of its party, acting against the most explicit expression of the popular will, acting against the advice of the best Imperialists, sanctioned the importation of Chinese coolies into the South African mines. It is not to be supposed that they would have done this merely for Dr Harris's £10,000. But there were certainly other South African mine-owners who were at once equally generous and more discreet. It is further to be noted, as we have already observed, that the Liberal Party, though it won the election of 1906 almost entirely on the issue of Chinese Labour, refused to allow a division on this issue to take place, and entered into friendly negotiations with the mine-owners, negotiations which assured that the Chinese should not be returned until they had done their work in reducing the wages of the Kaffirs.

Another case in which the influence of rich subscribers to the Party Funds upon the policy of the party can be very distinctly traced is in connection with the perennial Drink Problem. In no instance, perhaps, is it so clear that the talk about the "will of the people" deciding things is an elaborate piece of humbug. There are several possible policies in relation to the drink trade – municipalisation, for instance, and free trade – which the people are never allowed to hear of, much less to vote for. The only issue ever presented to the people is between Mr Balfour's Licensing Bill, which meant in effect the endowment of brewing and distilling firms out of public funds, and Mr Asquith's Licensing Bill, which meant a system of irritating restrictions upon the drinking habits of the people, restrictions leading logically to ultimate prohibition. The alternative of breaking the drink monopoly either by public ownership or by free private competition was never put before the nation at all.

Why was this? Simply because the two political parties need the money of rich men to conduct the sham fight upon which their own prestige and salaries depend. The policy must therefore be one that will attract some particular section of the rich class.

The Conservative Party relies largely upon the subscriptions of wealthy brewers and distillers, who are generally the owners of tied houses. Hence the policy of Mr Balfour's Licensing Bill. The Liberal Party flings its net wider. Some of its subscribers are men who live by manufacturing non-alcoholic drinks. Their interest in the suppression of alcoholic drinks is obvious. Others are interested in the grocery trade (whose organisation is closely connected with the party machinery), and live by selling alcoholic drinks retail. The fewer public-houses there are, the more uncomfortable they are, the less hours they are open, the more restrictions are imposed upon them, the more drink will these men sell. It is obviously to the interest of a grocery business that the public-houses in its neighbourhood should be closed. Note, then, how the grocery business stands with the "Liberal" Party.

Finally, the Liberal Caucus appeals to those rich men who have a fad for regulating the beverages of their neighbours, who do their best by means of their economic power to prohibit the sale of drink among their tenants or their employees, and who would gladly use political power to prohibit it everywhere else.

So it comes about that, while a sane policy which would discourage drunkenness (especially the degraded kind of drunkenness characteristic of the slums, the true name of which is drugging), while allowing normal men to get good liquor under decent conditions, would undoubtedly command the support of the people, it is just the one thing that the people are never allowed to consider. Their decision is only between the brewer and the cocoa-manufacturer. Not unnaturally, they usually prefer the brewer.

It must not be supposed that the Liberal politicians themselves are in the least degree more teetotal than their Conservative opponents. Most of them have quite an adequate taste in alcohol. But that the game may be carried on, money is needed. And the two organisations agree to appeal to different sections of the plutocracy. Thus the paymasters of the politicians are in this sense more sincere than the politicians are. They do want something in the way of legislation or administration, while the politicians want nothing but their salaries. The effectiveness of the two is proportional to their sincerity.

V

# THE CONTROL OF ELECTIONS

## The Party Caucus

E NOW RETURN to the machinery by which elections are determined. Before one can understand this one must understand that mysterious entity, the "Central Office."

What is the Central Office? It is not representative of the people. It is not even representative of the active members of the Party. These active members dispersed throughout their clubs are represented at the conferences of the National Liberal Federation and the National Union of Conservative Associations. These bodies pass resolutions and define policies; but nothing that they do has the smallest effect on practical politics until it has been ratified by the Central Office.

The Central Office is the medium of communication between the governing group on the Front Benches and the local party organisations throughout the country. These local organisations themselves do not represent very adequately the rank and file of the parties; they are composed of the most enthusiastic partisans (a small proportion of the community), and are largely dominated by the local rich men who help to keep them going. These men often covet seats in Parliament and work the local organisation with the object of obtaining them. Yet, unrepresentative as they often are, and controlled by local plutocracy, the local organisations are too democratic to be trusted under such a system as ours with the reality of political power. The Central Office exists to keep them in order.

At the head of the Central Office is an official nominated by the Governing Group. He is in close touch with the Whips, and, through them, with the Leader. He wisely leaves a certain amount of discretion to the local organisations in things not essential. But, where his intervention is required, as, for example, where a local organisation is disposed to stand by a man who takes an independent attitude, or where a man unacceptable to the Front Bench is nominated, he interferes, and his interference is usually successful, for in truth his power, though hidden, is immense.

For he holds the purse-strings. Through his hands pass all those huge secret sums of which we have already spoken. It is in his power to give or to withhold these; and they are constantly withheld from members who do not satisfactorily toe the party line. It is also he who makes arrangements with the subscribers to the Party Funds – arrangements of which the Leader is conventionally supposed to know nothing, though he obediently carries them out.

In fact, the Central Office, though by no means the most really powerful factor in our politics, is the hinge upon which everything else depends. Through it the politicians master the constituencies.

## The Selection of Candidates

We have already said that under a really democratic system of representation members of Parliament would be chosen freely by their constituents, probably in most cases from among their own number. In many cases they would be elected by acclamation. In others there might be a contest. But in the final resort it would be the man most thoroughly trusted by his fellow-citizens of that particular district who would become the member. It is clear that this does not happen now.

How do men get elected to Parliament? There are normally two processes. Sometimes the richest man in a particular locality interests himself in what is called "politics," and subscribes largely to the funds of the local organisation, sometimes paying all its expenses out of his own purse. In such a case he naturally becomes all-important to the local politicians, and if he cares to contest the seat he is, subject to confirmation by the machine—as we shall see when we deal with the process in the next section—chosen as candidate. This arrangement obviously implies wealth as a necessary condition of entrance into politics, and affords no guarantee whatever that the man chosen will really represent his constituents. It is, however, in practice probably less mischievous than the other and commoner course of procedure.

When a man has no special local connections, or when his political preferences do not accord with those of the locality to which his connections bind him, he must approach the Central Office, directly or indirectly, and ask them to find him a seat. If he is a rich man he will put down a subscription which will be paid into the secret treasury of the Party, and the seat found for him will, other things being equal, vary in security with the amount of the said subscription.* If, on the other hand, the man is poor, he will show himself active in political work, make speeches for other men, write articles in reviews, and generally force himself upon the notice of his patrons as a useful gladiator. If he can get a private secretaryship to a politician or in any other way connect himself with the Governing Group, his path will be all the smoother, and such action be thought more normal if he is a lawyer; for lawyers are at once recognised as advocates, offered the largest salaries (within and without the House), and further find men of their calling to be already the nucleus of Parliament. They are the most serviceable tools of the party bosses. Such an apprentice to the game will be generally sent in the first instance to fight some hopeless seat. If he shows himself a good candidate and makes himself agreeable to the leaders, a more hopeful seat is subsequently found for him. His poverty is no obstacle to his success, so long as he is submissive to the machine, for the Fortunatus Purse of the Party Funds is placed unreservedly at his disposal. But the sacrifice of his freedom (and honour) is the condition of his securing these advantages. If, by some accident, a junior actually elected so misunderstands his position as to ask a question or move a motion on some point affecting the machine, he is usually reminded—by an "independent" but wealthy colleague—that his

---

* Occasionally a rich but stupid man is duped, an apparently "safe" seat being offered him as against a really large sum of money, when the salaried officials of the two machines have already winked at a third independent candidature.

ability to fight his seat again depends upon the will of a secret Caucus, and of those by whose money that Caucus is kept going.

It must, of course, be remembered that local political organisations are, as will be described in a moment, no more than the old stock "Tory" or "Radical" stagers of the locality. Such men, though usually honest according to their lights, are completely the dupes of the professional politicians in London, and always insist on "loyalty to the party" as the first condition of confidence. This condition nullifies all others. For, once he is pledged to do nothing that may injure the party, a candidate can cheerfully pledge himself to almost anything else, well knowing that if the measure he is pledged to support is inconvenient to the Front Benches, he will either have no chance of voting on it, or his vote will be rendered harmless and ineffective by the subsequent shelving of the question. If in the last resort he is forced to break his word and vote against what he is pledged to vote for, he can always plead that to have redeemed his pledge would have endangered the Government; and by the eager "Liberals" or "Unionists" who make up local political Committees such a plea will generally be accepted. Even if he is so unusually unlucky as to fail to satisfy the local organisation on a particular point, they are, once he has been their member, almost powerless to get rid of him. To do so would be to cause a scandal, to divide the party, and to run the risk of handing over the seat to "the enemy"—as the dupes of one set of politicians innocently call the dupes of these politicians' confederates.

If any man ventures to run independently of the two political caucuses, the difficulties in the way of his success are enormous. Generally he is severely hampered for want of money, while his official opponents have not only an inexhaustible fund to draw upon, but a fund whose sole purpose is the financing *not* the winning of elections. Also, though a majority of voters may actually prefer him to any other candidate, they are often afraid to vote for him, lest by so doing they should "waste" their votes: for under an absurd and dishonest arrangement, which the machine carefully preserves, no second ballot is allowed. An impartial observer may be pardoned for thinking that, even under this system a man could hardly waste his vote more thoroughly than by giving it to the nominee of the political bosses, who, when he is once elected, must regard himself as the servant not of his constituents, but of the caucus. But British electors are not always impartial observers, and there is no doubt that the hypnotic effect of continual assurances that an independent candidate "cannot win" operates powerfully against him. Votes promised some days before the poll are in such cases continually revoked at the last moment under the influence of this "fear of wasting a vote."

Thus it will be seen that only three types of men find it normally possible to get into Parliament. First, local rich men who can dominate the local political organisation. Secondly, rich men from outside who have suborned the central political organisation. Thirdly, comparatively poor men who are willing, in consideration of a seat in Parliament and the chances of material gains which it offers, to become the obedient and submissive servants of the caucus.

## An Election

It will be attempted in this division to describe not why, but how, that wheel of the machine which is called "the local Caucus," the agency of the Machine in a constituency, works towards an election from start to finish.

Some recapitulation of what has already been read will be necessary, but no comment need be made on it, still less my criticism: a description is enough.

The two Front Benches have at their disposal a large organisation maintained by salaried officials whose object it is to decide what men shall stand for what constituencies. Each of these organisations is approached, and lays itself out for approach, on two sides: first by those who desire to become Members of Parliament; secondly, by the local bodies that must confirm the choice of a candidate.

The decision of the Salaried Machine Officials as to who shall stand for where is guided of course by many considerations. A wealthy man who has purchased the right to stand must of course be considered first; men already noted at the Universities for their connection with party organisation there, and their power of public speaking in connection with it, have an obvious claim. Heredity is a claim. A man, the son or connection of a prominent politician or wealthy political family, a Cecil,[20] a Howard, a Churchill, or a Rothschild, will be accepted as of right. A multitude of considerations enter here which we need not detail.

Men whose poverty renders them of no immediate importance, but whose gifts of advocacy are worthy of enlistment, will be given for their first trial (as we have already pointed out) places which the officials of the double machine have decided to be "safe" for the "side" opposed to that for which the neophyte is put up. His defeat and the energy he puts into the struggle earn him a right to a better chance next time.

Men of strong local influence, or possessed of private or valuable information, are of course welcomed—and so forth.

But one common test is applied: the men so chosen must be prepared to defend *not only an existing programme* settled between the various officials and professional politicians, but *any future decision* which their superiors may feel inclined to take. That is understood more or less clearly by the candidates so chosen: the more clearly the better their chance for promotion. A man of no powers, but of doubtful obedience, who might be tempted (were he elected) to speak for those who elected him, is offered the most hopeless opportunities until a few elections shall have schooled him.

Turn now to the local body.

In the constituencies the local machine depends upon considerable though dwindling bodies of sincere public feeling. You have not in the provinces that connivance and collusion between supposed opponents which is the essence of the central direction at Westminster. The local "prominent Liberals" are usually men of a really different type from the local "prominent Conservatives." The mass of the people, of course, care little for the "prominent Liberals" and "prominent Conservatives" whose business it is to approach the machine and discover a candidate for it. . . . But a few dozen men interested in such subjects surround the local bigwigs of either caucus, meet for the purpose of "electing" them to be "Presidents," "Treasurers," and so forth of the local caucus.

We say "a few dozen"; it is never a hundred, and there are many constituencies where it is not twenty or thirty. The local bigwigs thus "elected" by their local dependents and satellites form the "official Liberal" organisation and the "official Conservative" organisation: the word "official" here signifying "recognised by the salaried officials of the central machine at Westminster, and by the professional politicians to whom those officials owe their appointment and livelihood."

Upon the approach of an election, or perhaps some time before, the "official organisation" "deputes" that one of its members who most loves this form of activity, and who has most leisure, to go up to London and see the salaried officials of the machine. He goes up to London, perhaps two or three others go up with him; the interview takes place (we are talking here of course only of seats not already provided with a candidate or sitting member intending to continue in Parliament); they have no one ready, and ask for someone "on the list" to be "sent down," or perhaps they suggest a local man who has spent money largely in the constituency; and if he has agreed to vote for anything the machine may suggest, he is confirmed by the machine. More commonly in the case of a vacancy it is the Official at Westminser who nominates the man; but though nominated, he is not yet the "official prospective candidate." Before he can be called by that title he must present himself to the little local clique and be "accepted by the official (blue or green) organisation." Now and then (it is exceedingly rare, and is the exception that proves the rule) the choice thus made is so appalling that the little local clique is frightened of it; in ninety-nine cases out of a hundred they do as they are bid, and the gentleman becomes the "official prospective candidate" of the blues or the greens, as the case may be. He may, if there is time and if he is wealthy, "nurse" the constituency; that is, provide material advantages for the benefit of the electorate; but, though he may "benefit" the electors to his heart's content so far as *amount* is concerned, he must be wary enough to stop a certain *time* before the election takes place: otherwise it is bribery. The length of this time is of course not fixed, but depends on the whim of the judge, should an election petition be tried. Six months is perhaps the maximum.

From a fortnight to ten days before the election takes place the "campaign" opens; a set of points are provided for the candidate by the professional politicians, and he has to defend them in public meetings: questions are put to him which he must answer as best he may. If a movement of public opinion is observable on matters *outside* the brief which he has been chosen to defend, he is expected to turn this movement aside and if possible to destroy it, but it is permitted that he should, in extreme cases of spontaneous popular excitement, pledge himself with a view to his return, though always on the understanding that he is bound to the machine and not to the constituency. He is expected to break those pledges always in the spirit, and even, if necessary, in the letter, after his return to Westminster: the complete ignorance of the populace upon the rules of Parliament makes the task an easy one.

As the day of the poll approaches, the candidates are "nominated"; that is, nomination papers are handed in bearing the names of certain of his supporters. *The nomination is not accepted unless he can bring with him and pay down in cash a large sum of money, equivalent to the full year's income of a well-paid skilled artisan.* This, of course, is not the whole amount of the entrance fee: the full expenses can hardly be kept at less than £400, average in their avowed or legal amount £1000, and come in reality (if all be counted) to nearly double that sum.

A day or two before the election takes place, that excitement which the national character finds and delights in where any doubtful event is approaching lends great heartiness to the unreal struggle: unreal so far as any difference of principle is concerned, but commonly very real in the conflicting ambitions of the two candidates.

The last night or two before the poll is a debauch of mere excitement upon either side, called "a rally," the intensity of which is often a gauge as to whether a few hesitating voters have been drawn into the whirlpool on the one side or the other. But its main purpose is not persuasion, but ritual; it is very expensive, and there is some finessing as to the bespeaking of halls, etc.

Meanwhile a number of workers of the poorest classes, who by legal theory give their services gratuitously, are engaged in personally interviewing every elector and getting him to say that he will vote for their "side." The majority pledge themselves to *both* sides, as indeed courtesy demands; but a certain proportion answer "yes" to the one side and "no" to the other. As is always the case where large numbers of human beings are being estimated, an average can be struck, and the average of these stubborn souls is fairly fixed; to estimate the results of the "canvass," as it is called (it is endowed with an elaborate system of checks and counter-checks) a certain percentage is taken off all the pledges: doubtfuls are added to one's opponent's canvass, and the result is thought to be, and often is, a rough indication of how the poll will go.

On the day of the poll the voters cannot, of course, be expected to register their opinions–for, as a rule, opinions are not at stake–nor even to fulfil their pledges; a vast and (again) an *expensive* organisation for getting at each voter personally and bringing him to the poll is set to work. The opportunity of a ride in a motor car or a carriage is not without its influence, and the mere pestering by the "workers" is of great effect. Were it not for this costly effort the proportion of those who vote would be negligible in most constituencies. It is, of course, essential to the life of the Party System that the numbers should be fairly equal on either of the sham "sides," taking the country as a whole.

Therefore, to win by 10 per cent. of the electorate in any one constituency is an enormous majority; to win by 5 per cent. a solid and satisfactory one; to win by 2 per cent, does not mean that the seat is "safe," but the election is hardly called "close"; blue or green gets the larger number of crosses, and duly goes off to Westminster to vote for anything whatsoever that the machine may give him orders to vote for during the next few years.

No mention has been made of what is called the "organisation," with its local salaried officials, noting the removal of every elector, checking the names, places on the list, residences of all, and so forth. That type of work may be easily imagined. Oddly enough it is commonly performed (though at a wage) by one of those men, common in the provinces, who sincerely believe in the reality of the differences between the professional politicians. Their simple faith is one of the anomalies of the system.

Thus does the party engine work at the constituency end of its activities, and thus is the personnel of the House of Commons determined. It helps to explain that personnel.

## The Selection of Programmes

If the selection of members has, of course, been taken completely out of the hands of the people, quite equally so has been the selection of the "programme" of which they are supposed to ask the electors' approval, but which, as a fact, official candidates must depend on as on a brief.

In a really democratic system, as has been pointed out, the initiative would come from the people. They would ask for certain alterations in the law, and would send men to Parliament to express their wishes.

The demand by the electors would come first, and the declarations of the candidate would merely embody that demand. Under such a system programmes would naturally vary from constituency to constituency according to the special needs and grievances of the locality; but some demands would be common to all, because the grievance to be redressed was felt by the whole nation.

Now, as a matter of fact, nothing of the kind happens.

Two programmes are drawn up by the politicians, usually after consultation with each other, and between these two alone are the voters asked to choose.

No subject not mentioned in either programme, however much the people may desire to raise it, can be effectually raised. No solution of any problem, except the two prescribed solutions, however much the people might prefer it, can ever be really discussed. Nothing is left to the people but to choose the least of two evils.

It is true that in framing these programmes the politicians have their eyes on votes. But the vote-catching of politicians is a matter of arbitrary arrangement; it has nothing to do with any national demand. One side is to bid for the votes of Churchmen; the other of Nonconformists. One is to secure the support of publicans; the other of teetotalers. But the question to be answered is framed by the politicians. And to frame the question is to go a long way towards framing the answer.

It was not always so; at least not to the same extent. Just as the control of the House of Commons over the Ministry has weakened, just as the control of the electors over their members has weakened, so has the initiative of the people in legislation weakened.

As an illustration of this, compare the Free Trade movement of the 'forties with the Tariff Reform movement. We do not propose to discuss the question of the relative merits of Free Trade and Protection.* But this may be fairly said, that Free Trade was forced upon the legislature by the urgent demand of a section of the people – a minority perhaps, but still a section. Tariff Reform, on the other hand, had its rise in no such demand. There were always, it is true, in this country a considerable number of convinced Protectionists. Some were old-fashioned Tories who regretted the repeal of the Corn Laws.[21] Others were economists who had studied the Continental and American advocates of Protection, and agreed with them. Others were working men who believed that the foreigner had got their job. But these men, though one continually met them, were politically utterly negligible. Suddenly a Cabinet Minister, a member of the governing group, spoke and declared for Protection. On the instant, men who had never in their lives before doubted the validity of Free Trade, but who happened to be professional politicians, suddenly appeared as convinced Protectionists, while crowds of their satellites and would-be replacers at once followed suit.

But there is no matter for wonder in this phenomenon. It is normal to the working of the machine, for the machine presupposes that popular opinion shall have no initiative.

There is no machinery by which, at the present time, the people can raise a particular political question, however intensely it may

---

* It is indeed a question concerning which the two authors of this book decidedly disagree.

interest them, unless it is included in the programme of one or other of the political parties. They can indeed obtain pledges from candidates; but such pledges, as we have seen, are perfectly valueless; for, though a man may be pledged to vote for a particular measure, he cannot vote for it unless it is brought before Parliament and a division taken on it; and it has already been shown that the Front Benches can generally prevent a division on any inconvenient question, and even if a division is taken, can prevent the matter going any further. Thus, even supposing, no small supposition, that the elected member is honestly desirous of keeping his promise and carrying out the wishes of his constituents, he will generally find it impossible to do so. The Front Benches, by their control of the House of Commons, control also the effective programmes submitted to the electors.

Even if the solution of some question is so urgently demanded by the electors (or far more often by the rich men whose money is at the back of the official parties) that the Government cannot ignore it, the voters are not allowed to choose their own solution, but only to vote for one of two solutions put forward by the Front Benches. We have already given one example of this—the Drink Question. The people are from time to time allowed to choose between the suppression of public-houses and their endowment out of public money, but they are not allowed to vote for any other policy, least of all are they allowed to vote, as they certainly would vote if they got the chance, for the removal of some or all of the intricate and mostly senseless regulations which interfere at every point with the habits and festivities of the poor. The numerous Education Bills, drafted not to satisfy the people whose children are to be educated, but solely to gain the support of sectarian leaders of all kinds—men who would as soon think of sending their children to be educated in Nigeria as at a public elementary school—afford another example.

To take cases where the demand comes from a section at any rate of the populace: the two Front Benches decided last November that the reversal of the Osborne Judgment should not be among the issues presented to the electors for decision; they secretly agreed that payment of members should side-track the demand of the workers. The Labour Party of course gave way; the Front Benches have won.

In regard to the Unemployed, the people are not and will not be allowed to vote for or against the Right to Work Bill, though they might be allowed to consider Mrs Webb's[22] policy of imprisoning working men in compounds until they consent to work for the rich. It is more likely, however, that such a proposal would, like the Children's Bill and the Prevention of Crimes Bill, be carried over their heads as a "non-controversial measure." "Non-controversial measures," it may be explained, include all violently unpopular proposals for the oppression of the poor, which happen in no way to affect the professional politicians.

For with the loss of initiative the people have also lost all right of veto, so that not only are they unable to frame the programme which their representative is to carry into effect, not only can their demands, even if their representative is pledged to them, be entirely neglected, but the most detested of measures, for which there is no shadow of mandate, which were never mentioned at the previous election, may be passed into law, and the electorate is utterly powerless to secure their repeal. Even though they should punish their member for voting for such measures by rejecting him at the next election, his successor, the representative of the other team, will probably lack the will, and will certainly lack the power to undo the work, if that work is approved by the Front Benches. The Licensing Clauses of the Budget, which are certainly unpopular, but which the "Conservative" team undoubtedly intend to continue when by mutual arrangement their turn of office comes, afford an excellent example of this.

It is clear then that, despite all the elaborate machinery of polling-booths and ballot-papers, despite all the frenzied appeals to "the popular will" which are the staple of political eloquence at election times, the people have neither the power to make Parliament pass the laws that they want nor to prevent it from passing the laws that they dislike. The whole power of legislation has passed to that Standing Committee of Professional Politicians which is called in the House of Commons "The Two Front Benches."

# VI

# THE DEFENCE

The Excuses

HE WHOLE of this book so far has consisted in a criticism of the Party System. It is well for the sake of right judgment to consider at the close what may be (and is privately) said in its favour by those who make their living off it. What excuses do they offer? First this:

States, as all the world knows, and as those who know the world least are never tired of informing us, are organic things, not mechanical. You cannot make a State: it has to grow.

The English State at the present moment, or, to speak more accurately, the British State (excluding of course Ireland, the new countries, and the dependencies) has enjoyed a peculiarly unbroken continuity of institutions. Not a peculiarly unbroken continuity compared with many States in history; but, during the last 150 years at least, a peculiarly unbroken one, compared with the great States of Europe, its rivals.

Among the other institutions of Britain which have been developed during this comparatively long period of unbroken continuity stands the Party System. Under its machinery, acting according to its rules, England, until she began to experience her recent embroilments and anxieties, prospered. She was, until recently, the wealthiest nation in the world; and in the full military sense of military strength, wherein defence is a main part of the problem, she was almost the strongest. Men of high capacity have continually succeeded one another as a product of the Party System, and in general, being an institution in a State whose institutions have been so continuous, it should remain.

This is the first and most plausible excuse which its beneficiaries make in favour of the Party System. There is attached to it a converse excuse of almost equal effect which stands thus:

In a State of ancient institution—indeed, in any State—you must not lightly destroy an institution, for when you have destroyed it you cannot with ease replace it by another institution. The political institutions of men are not theories, they are things. Destroy the monarchy, for instance, of a despotic society, and you are bound to supply the gap which it has left by some other definite and powerful organ of government, concrete because it is human, and because it is human necessarily subject to error and to vice. "Leave well alone" should therefore be a standing motto, so far as primary institutions are concerned, with every patriotic man. Unless you have some clear alternative capable of concrete expression, and certainly capable of giving as good a result as the institution you propose to overthrow, then an attack upon it is anarchic and profoundly unwise.

But apart from these two, which are the main excuses offered by the Professional politicians in favour of the Party System today, its apologists can draw up an abstract series of arguments in its favour.

The Party System, properly worked, reposes essentially upon this doctrine: that to every question there must be a positive and a negative answer: with every policy suggested by a statesman we must roughly and in the main acquiesce, or we must roughly and in the main dissent from it. An all-powerful Executive, or even an Executive which submits to the check that can be given by representative bodies or by other organs in the State, affords no opportunity for the discussion, and the balance for and against, of any policy. The Party System is therefore better than an unchecked or but partially checked Executive; and indeed it was its superiority over such forms of Executive which was the boast of Englishmen over the Continent a hundred years ago.

On the other hand (would say both the beneficed defender of the Party System and the Don who is happily ignorant of intrigue), actual *government* by a deliberative body, or even the granting of a supreme power of veto and check to a deliberative body, is in practice impossible. A deliberative body, in proportion to its excellence in its deliberative character, is incapable of initiative and of directly expressed will. The best thing we can do for the State, therefore, is to preserve a system under which, while one body of men shall be tempted, in order to preserve and obtain large salaries and power, to put forward a policy which they believe to be agreeable to the commonwealth, and which at the same time they know is so debatable as to require open discussion, another body, commanding followers fairly equal in numbers, shall be present as advocates upon the other side to help decide the issue.

In many policies the nation will be so much at one that the play of the two parties will not be called upon; as, for instance, in the determination to grant Old Age Pensions in 1907. In other cases details only, not general policies, are at stake, and for this the kind of debate known in the House of Commons as the "Committee stage" of a Bill amply provides. But for the very largest issues in national policy nothing can work for more open or more thorough discussion, and for a more proper appreciation of the national mind, than the presence in numbers, not too unequal, of two sets of debaters, sent by the electorate to Westminster for the purpose of discussing some great subject which has been put forward as a policy by one or the other of the leading teams. Such a debate we are having (the apologists for the Party System would say) upon the great and important national question of Protection *versus* Free Trade. And the reiterated arguments, examples, rhetorical appeals (the whole criticism and flux to which the policy of Free Trade and its opposite are subjected by the Party System) proves the superiority of that system to any other method of government.

Again, the Party System provides (it has often been pointed out) an alternative government. The alternative government is potentially there; no violence, no breach with the past is necessary to establish under our happy institutions even the greatest change in the conduct of the nation. Had a party system been working, for instance, in France when one set of French politicians decided upon religious schism, the electorate would have been consulted upon that issue; and when they had decided in favour of schism or against it, a body of men trained in government and willing to express the views of the majority of the electors—or rather of their deputies—would have been ready instantly to take the place of the other body whose policy had lost the confidence of the nation.

Many other minor arguments may be advanced—by such as are interested in it—to defend the Party System.

It may be urged, for instance, that in England—whatever is the case with other countries—a faint line of cleavage really dividing the nation into two (but providentially not so deep as to wound its unity) is to be discovered. There is your English Liberal type, and your English Conservative type, your Chapel man and your Church man, and to this line of cleavage which is a reality, the reality of the Party System corresponds.

Yet another minor argument resides in this: that with the Party System you can get an organisation and equipment of the electorate which you could never get without such a discipline. Thus we may compare the percentage of voters in contested elections in England with the percentage that come to the poll abroad, and the advantage in our favour may be laid to the door of the Party System.

Finally—and this, as it is the least rational and the most ignorant, is with politicians the most powerful argument of all—the Party System works not only well, but *better* than any corresponding system among our great rivals. The position we hold among the nations, the happiness and the content of our masses, our power of immediate and irresistible offence in the vindication of our national rights or desires, our sober, successful, and profound social reforms which are the admiration of the universe, have been the product of the Party System; and even if something theoretically better, nay, something demonstrably better in the concrete, could be presented to us, we should be foolish indeed to abandon that which has made of this country everything that the citizens of any country can possibly desire.

Now, against these excuses it is fortunately not difficult to open batteries which leave them in ruins.

If we take the various points mentioned—and they fairly cover the ground of those who still apologise for our moribund parliamentary methods—they can be riddled one after the other with an ease that makes one almost ashamed to undertake the task. Let us proceed, as is only fair in such cases, from the weakest to the strongest, and consider the arguments just stated in the opposite order to that wherein we have laid them down.

The last argument, which certainly has had until lately the greatest force and which is still not without its power in what are called "the residential suburbs" of our great towns; the argument which in itself was worth, until recently, more than all the others put together, is today based, where it exists, upon those two characters which, in any society, are most directly and immediately ruinous of its prosperity: ignorance and vanity. Nothing but an appalling ignorance can make those who live under the Party System today believe that the State has today the strength it used to have for offence against foreign enemies; that it holds the economic position it held a generation ago; that the condition of our enormous population of very poor is regarded with anything but pity and horror by the more contented peoples of continental Europe; that our hasty and incomplete social reforms, our method of raising and our present necessities for spending the public revenue, are models for other nations. Even if ignorance permitted a man to hold such fantastic opinions, nothing but vanity could permit him to hold them untroubled. Though a man should never have travelled a mile out of his own country, nor be acquainted with a single foreign language, nor (what is perhaps more important) be capable of one sound judgment upon any foreign thing he saw or any foreign word he read, yet short of a most disastrous and diseased vanity he must know that a complete satisfaction with such a society as he sees round him in the great cities that are the typical polities of Britain, is below the normal standard of human political achievement.

Though he have no history, and be unable to compare the modern wretchedness with the happiness of the past, yet mere instinct and the common conscience of man must, unless he is positively blinded by vanity, teach him that something is very ill with England today.

True, it would be inept to lay at the door of one such institution as the Party System the enormous evils from which Britain increasingly suffers, and their increase at a rate which seriously menaces her future. But that is not the point. The point is that to argue from the excellence of conditions in England today to the excellence of the Party System is to argue from a falsehood to a nonsensical result. The social and political conditions in England today are not good, but bad: they are bad compared with our own remote past, bad compared with those of our great rivals, and bad compared with that standard of tolerable conditions which all men carry in them and which is something very different from and much lower than any ideal of a perfect society.

As for the pretension that the parties do correspond to a real though not a deep division between two kinds of English thought, it deserves more careful examination.

In the origin of the Party System that system corresponded to a very real and a very deep division. The system itself was run by an aristocracy and run more or less corruptly—very corruptly as far as individual statesmen were concerned. But these individual statesmen were the spokesmen of two great bodies of really divided opinion: the one inherited from Jacobite loyalty, the other from the Whig revolution. Doctor Johnson was not a dupe, he was not an ignorant man, above all he was not a fraud. He was a man very learned, one acquainted with all kinds of his fellows, intensely national and gloriously sincere: and Doctor Johnson did hate a Whig. Two very distinct philosophies once animated the two parties, and the distinction between these philosophies retained some vigour till the last quarter of the nineteenth century. The echoes of those opposed political philosophies have been heard by many men now living. Indeed, it is possible to forgive an elderly man, sincere, informed, and courageous, who still attaches some sort of meaning to the supposed differences between the party leaders. He may have a knowledge that in our moment their play is a pure humbug, but he can remember a generation in which some sort of ideal contest, or at any rate the savour of it, still remained.

But if we are talking of conditions as they exist here and now, then we must admit, in proportion to our information of what the political world is and of how its sham battles are as a matter of fact fought today, that not the memory, not the savour of a real distinction remains.

There are still a number of Tory squires in the countrysides, but the party which they reluctantly support does not pretend to represent them.

There are still a number of honest and elderly middle class Liberals lingering in the suburbs of our great towns, but the party for which they vote (those of them who do not call themselves "liberal Unionists") is not fighting their battles.

As for the mass of the people whom once these divisions also affected in some degree, they affect it now no longer. There is no division, not even the adumbration of a division, there is no line, not even the vaguest dotted line, which marks off, in psychology, manners, inherited tradition, or practice of daily life, a wage-earner who votes for Jones from a wage-earner who votes for Smith. The distinction imposed by official candidates is for the mass of workers absolutely unreal; and the individuals in the mass of workers by an overwhelming majority would, if they were asked, say so in so many words. They vote thus and thus apathetically, with no hope that any result will come to them from their vote, and they vote with no feeling of intimate sympathy between the philosophy of the candidate they support and their own philosophy; and that for a very good reason: the candidate whom they may support, whether he stands pledged to obey the one set of leaders or the other, is defending no philosophy at all. The argument from a supposed real division of the people upon the lines of the parties simply will not hold water.

Nor will the next arguments in the series hold water. It is not true that the Party System provides an alternative Government ready to take the helm at a moment's notice after a great change. Of all systems in modern Europe it provides such a Government *least.*

Let a violent Catholic reaction take place in France; let a strong Particularist movement appear in Italy; let self-government be granted to Ireland, – and to take over the management of changed conditions capable men could immediately be found. But the Party System in this country depends upon the very conception that there cannot be any vital or considerable change. All the working of the party men and all their system of living upon the taxes is bound up with the necessity that the point of policy chosen to divide them shall never be a vital one; and that in their method of daily life, the very set of drawing rooms they frequent, there shall be no differences between Hanky and Panky whatsoever. A sudden change requiring an alternative Government is something which the Party System has taught the public to regard as wholly out of nature. Its appearance in a foreign country, however fruitful, is put by our party politicians before our populace as something alien and comic; and such men as really do desire a change, in religion (as some we could name), in economic arrangement (as the Socialists), in national arrangement (as the Irish), are treated by the Party System and its supporters with a violence of vituperation, a swift, determined and calculating offensive which give the lie to all the foolish and hypocritical talk about the deliberation and sobriety of our public life.

The same objection applies to the claim that the Party System permits of free and full debate upon the main issues before a nation: it does nothing of the kind. It permits of full and free debate only upon such subjects as the two allied teams called "the Government" and "the Opposition" have decided to have debated. Now and then, indeed, an intriguer of prominence, for some purpose of his own, breaks the rules of the game. He occupies perhaps a position high enough to be able to do so with advantage. This was the case when Mr Gladstone launched Home Rule without consulting the greater part of his colleagues, let alone his nominal opponents: it was the case, again, when Mr Joseph Chamberlain launched Protection.

But even these real issues, once launched, are seized upon by the Party System and turned, by a process of digestion, as it were, into unreal issues in the shortest possible time. When once it was appreciated that the House of Lords would not pass Home Rule, the arguments for and against that policy were debated with all the professional rant of the play-actors upon our dull parliamentary stage. There was no conviction in their accents, and for the most of them no definite desire to arrive at a result, save the putting into office – that is, the giving of power and wealth to one of the two teams.

If anyone doubt this, let him discover the attitude of the Irish in Ireland upon the question. He will find that the so-called "Unionist" Party is regarded in precisely the same light as its pretended opponents. Every Irishman you will ever meet discussing the advantages his country has obtained during the last thirty years will talk with a complete impartiality of this Act, that policy, this personality, that blunder; sometimes oblivious of and always indifferent to the supposed party divisions at Westminster. So false is it that the Party System affords opportunity for full and reasoned debate upon great national issues, that not one great national issue since the repeal of the Corn Laws has obtained this supposed advantage. Not one piece of policy, however necessary, but, if it has become law, has become law by an agreement between the two sets of actors in the game. Where they have really disagreed the result has always been stalemate, and that for the very sufficient reason that a real and permanent victory upon either side would be the death of the system by which both sets of politicians obtain their bread-and-butter.

Finally, what are we to say with regard to the argument that the Party System, being an institution of this continuous and highly institutional country, should not lightly be tampered with?

As was said at the beginning of this chapter, that argument is a very powerful argument indeed. It appeals at once to the heart and to the head of every man who knows what a State is, and of every man who has any reverence for the past. There are innumerable examples to which this argument applies in modern England with more or less force. It is a strong plea for most of our ancient corporations; certainly for nearly all our ancient, and upon the whole innocuous, customs. It is a plea even for the maintenance of many definite and corporate institutions, ill-suited perhaps to the modern State, but possessing advantages of their own which, after reform, could never be supplied; but it is not an argument for the Party System, because the Party System, as an institution, has lost both the externals that bound it to the life of the State, and the internal vitality which gave it a real meaning.

The Party System is now neither a quaint and an innocuous re-
minder of the past, nor a corporate and living thing still possessed
of its identity and forming an integral part of the State.

It is not a mere symbol of our continuity, as are the wigs of
our judges, or the curious little jockey cap which some official
(whose name escapes us) carries at a high salary upon his head
when the King's assent to Bills is given in the House of Lords,*
or the archaic English and unnatural accent of the various rituals
affected by ministers of religion.

Nor does it, to turn from relics to living institutions, correspond to what the Inns of Court are in the organisation of our legal
system, or the collegiate arrangement of Oxford and Cambridge in
the organisation of our University life.

The Party System, in other words, insofar as it is an institution,
is an institution in the last stages of decay, but one which, since it
affects the greatest interests of the nation, is not innocuous; moreover, as it has long lost any true identity with its past, it is no longer
really alive. The necessity of being rid of it is like the necessity one
is under of being rid of a great dead body in one's neighbourhood
when it has begun to putrefy. The decay of party has already begun
to disturb the national life, and if we are not careful it may poison it–so far has its corruption proceeded–and yet so obstinately
do certain interests–mainly of a private nature and generally connected with salaries–persist in retarding its natural end.

We have indeed no need to concern ourselves further with the
excuses offered for a continuance of the machine. Nothing remains
in practical politics but for the practical politician to destroy the
Party System as rapidly and as thoroughly as may be.

There is no need of finding an alternative. The alternative is
there, underlying the evil. A free parliament, the ancient theory
of a national deliberative assembly, is ready to hand when the
encumbrance is got rid of. We do not need to frame some scheme
which shall supplant the Party System: all we have to do is to make
the Party System impossible; and that end will be accomplished

---

* Is it not the Master of the Horse?

when a sufficient number of men are instructed in its hypocrisies and follies, when the real and modern peril which it involves has been brought home to a sufficient number, and when men begin to ask for an opportunity to express their opinions at the polls. Light on the nasty thing and an exposure of it are all that is necessary. It stinks only because it has been so carefully masked and covered and its natural dissolution thereby checked.

It is with the object of exposing it that this book, which happily is but one of many vigorous contemporary efforts in the same direction, has been written.

One real obstacle does, however, remain to reform, and that is the strength of the only real support upon which the professional politicians and their now exhausted method can rely; and that real support is the attitude of the "Plain Man"–mainly of the lower middle classes–who, particularly in the suburbs of our great towns, is used by those professionals partly as a dupe and partly as an ally. Let us examine this person.

## The Real Support

Into all attempt at reform there enters an element which is the converse of mere criticism or of mere exposure, and which forms a necessary basis for any constructive work. That element is the element of popular need.

Unless the mass of the nation needs a reform, not only is there no necessity for the undertaking of a considerable change, but there is great difficulty in accomplishing it; and it is and has been the continual error of abortive schemes that they corresponded only to some need suggested by historical parallels or present in a contemporary few, but not felt by the general body of citizens. It is not true, so far as political arrangements at least are concerned, that the desires or the necessities of a small minority immediately or even gradually impose themselves upon the State. Opinion may indeed be gradually so imposed by persuasion, and a new philosophy propagated; but until the new idea is accepted, acts cannot follow, and political change is invariably accompanied by a general and widespread ill-ease, which ill-ease is the expression of a popular need.

That a need for change is felt in modern England with regard to the machinery by which a small number of co-opted men combine to govern the country in collusion is certain. But there is a body in which that need is not felt, and to which it does not apply. This body, which we have called "the Real Support" of the Party System, must now be examined.

We have seen in the preceding pages what excuses might be presented for the Party System of government by those several types of people who are directly interested in its continuance; and we have tried to appreciate the measure of sincerity which each such appeal would contain. Is there not perhaps a large and popular apology for the same thing, an apology that would proceed not from those interested in the maintenance of the system, but from those whom it governs, and (as the reformer would say) exploits?

Let us take a certain type of British elector, perhaps a business man or a shopkeeper or even an artisan, who, though by no means wholly duped by the Party System, yet lends it his support; and let us ask ourselves whether many such would not reply to the demand for reform somewhat as follows (*how* many would so reply we must discuss later):

"You have been careful to explain to me that a little group of men belonging to a class whose only common mark is wealth, reserve to themselves enormous salaries paid out of my pocket, and monopolise all the political power in the State, by the playing of an elaborate game. Their professions do not correspond with the true motives of the players, and the rules of this game do not concern the well-being of the body politic, but rather the maintenance of an even balance between two picked and chosen teams, which even balance is necessary to the proper conduct of any pastime, whether lucrative or merely entertaining.

"Well, I knew that already. I did not perhaps know all the details you have put before me, but in general I was acquainted with the nature of the business. It is not a fraud practised upon me; it is rather an admitted fiction necessary to the play of our institutions, and a fiction which I readily use.

"I do this for a number of reasons. I have a long tradition of it behind me; the accidents of the game afford me the best opportunity for a practical redress of grievances; it furnishes me with a mild excitement which is none the worse for being largely make-believe, and there is about it just as much reality as I feel inclined to put into my view of public life.

"For instance, I am quite anxiously in favour of the taxation of land values in towns, and would willingly sacrifice a week's holiday or pay a day's wages to see that reform put into practice; and you cannot deny that that half of the clique which calls itself 'Liberal' is at the present moment trying to put such a reform into practice, while the other half, their brothers, uncles, cousins, intimate friends, etc., who call themselves 'Unionists,' are on the whole resisting the reform.

"I feel about my politics what I feel about my religion: the necessity for clothing a few moderate and vague tendencies in strong and exaggerated language, and in a heavy and stiff ceremonial which I know does not correspond to any internal strictness of definition, but which affords me something concrete upon which I can repose.

"When I go to a public meeting and hear Lord Algernon Crape denouncing Mr Charles Anger for an assassin and a traitor, I know as well as you do that Lord Algernon Crape married last year Mr Charles Anger's sister, and that the two young men are really intimate friends. But I like that kind of thing in the ceremonial of my political religion. I am an Englishman; I like to see a prize-fight much more than to see a fight with lethal weapons; I like to read in books that I am a bold rider, that I love the sea, and that I indulge in fisticuffs—though of course I know very well that I can't ride, that the sea knocks me out, that I do not use my fists in quarrels, and that if I had to it would be extremely distasteful to me: it is fiction, but the fiction is good for me. Every nation and every society of men has its ritual and its convention, and ritual and convention of their nature involve make-believe.

"Then again, you are concerned to tell me that this clique of people are very rich, and, where large sums of money are concerned, very corrupt. You have pointed this out to me in rather more detail than I am accustomed to; but it is with this point as with the rest. I knew all about it before you were kind enough to explain it to me. I happen to like that kind of thing. What revolts me in the conduct of a State is not theft on a large scale by the few rich officials, but the acceptation of bribes on a small scale by the many poor officials. I feel instinctively that the second evil is much more practically dangerous to the State than the first.

"Mr Pompous, you tell me, made a new office with a salary of about £40 a week attached to it, stuck his mistress's nephew into it, and gave that nephew's brother a fantastic fee out of the taxes for some arbitration work in the Far East. You tell me that Mr Pompous was only able to pull off the double job by letting the money-lender, Mr Judaeus, suck dry the resources of such and such an Oriental district over which Mr Pompous' colleague and first cousin was the master through his position in the Cabinet; but, my dear sir, had I been in old Pompous' place, I should have acted in precisely that same fashion. In my own sphere I act in that fashion every day. I rather respect Pompous for having managed to hold his tongue and to control his face so well for so many years as to have arrived at a position where he can cheat on a really large scale. Meanwhile, I see that the system gives me the services of Pompous' brother-in-law for nothing. This chap inherited a couple of millions; what he wants is power and notoriety. He will never take a bribe, and he will give the State all the advantage of his ample leisure and vast opportunities.

"Best of all, with such a system Pompous and his gang will be absolutely merciless in punishing any corruption apparent in minor officials, and it is *that* kind of corruption, multiform, universal, and soon ineradicable, which poisons a State.

"Finally, I have noticed running through your criticism for reform one main note, which is that the Party System, apart from its falsehood and financial corruption, is especially to be condemned because it prevents any true representation of the popular will.

"Now, my dear sir, I have no sort of desire for the 'Representation of the Popular Will.' Phrases like that give me a headache. A machinery exists, an institution and traditions, which furnish me with a competent and regularly renewed set of men who look after the public weal. My forefathers have not, since the Middle Ages, concerned themselves with such abstractions as 'the popular will,' and though I often use the word 'represent' and the substantive 'representation,' I don't care a row of pins about either. I know very well that a violent and universal national feeling would be respected by the Party System, and it is only violent and universal feelings of the sort that the people as a whole need be concerned about.

"I might end by telling you this: I *like* to be governed by rich men. It makes me feel cosy. Perhaps that is because it rids me of any sense of responsibility and puts me vaguely into touch with luxuries I cannot enjoy. Anyhow, I like to be governed by rich men, and your Party System is precisely the sort of thing which rich men, when you give them their head, will develop."

That, put much more shortly and much less didactically, is what many such an elector, to whatever class he may belong, up and down England feels when he hears the Party System attacked; that is the instinctive reply of many such men. How many? Well, it is very difficult to answer that question.

Note that the professions of political faith which the average man will make, the man with two to five pounds a week coming into his house from a small business or employment, or from a skilled trade in which, let us say, his sons are helping him, are not identical with nor even closely connected with his political appetites and instincts. The same man who is delighted to denounce at a public meeting the rapacity of peers will be equally delighted to have as his chairman at the meeting some younger son of a peer who has just decided to call himself a Radical. And such a man will certainly support by his vote and influence any chance party hack against a representative of his own class who shall have made any real attempt to destroy the power of the plutocracy.

In general, it cannot be denied that the Party System, even in this its last moribund and putrescent phase, reposes upon certain habits of thought still persistent in sections of the middle classes and established artisans. When, in the near future, the thin shell still covering the nastiness of the fraud shall break, that part of the nation will be exceedingly annoyed and will blame everyone except the politicians for the bad smell; and one may conclude that no exposure, no appeal, and no criticism will have any real weight in this quarter, because, before they could have weight, routine, which is the main necessity of such lives, would have to disappear.

Upon what practical basis, then, can reform repose? To what instincts or needs can it appeal, and what co-operation will it discover in what fractions of the State?

The practical basis upon which reform must build, if the strength of the nation is to be maintained on its political side, is the basis of public utility.

Both within and without these islands there are tasks set for modern England which the Party System is wholly unable to accomplish.

It cannot meet our prompt, centralised, and lucid rivals abroad, notably the French and the Prussians. It cannot save the mass of the people from an increasing insecurity in their earnings, and economic conditions increasingly intolerable. In the first of these fields the Party System is beginning to make a dangerous fool of itself, alternately denying its own existence, and then, through some panicky move of its tawdry game, seriously weakening England in one or another department of her foreign or colonial policy. In the second of these fields it slowly tinkers: and even when a social reform is in the right direction, its pace is as a pace of one mile an hour where the rate of growth of the evil is as twenty miles an hour; either a social reform produced by the politicians is quite off the point (and this is the case nine times out of ten), or it is negligibly small, or it is hopelessly tardy, and comes too late, with a rush, and is not thought out at all. In both fields, foreign and domestic, the Party System must be superseded, or we shall drop behind our rivals.

That is the practical need to which we must appeal; and of the many fractions of the community to which we *can* appeal the two most important are the inarticulate and despairing mass which has hitherto never considered the governance of England as in any way concerning it, and the youth which is still deceived (though less and less deceived with every day) by the pretence of the professional politicians.

Motive power, however, will be lacking to any reform, unless men can be convinced that the failure of Parliament has led not only or merely to hypocrisy and a contemptible corruption, the degradation of public life and of public office, but also to real and tangible national peril.

## The Peril

The life of a great nation still in full activity, multitudinous, and even numerically increasing (though that last test is a poor one), is a difficult medium in which to express the perils which may threaten its society.

It is granted on every side that politics have become contemptible, and the political machine ridiculous or provocative of indignation, according to the temper of those who are compelled to observe it.

But this conviction is a very different thing from the conviction that such an evil is productive of direct and tangible danger to the State.

What happens in men's minds when they turn today with disgust from politicians is not so much to remember that the men whom they thus despise are still in theory the masters of the national fate, but to occupy themselves with the living industry and commerce and the living debates of true public opinion.

The State in which we live has no recent experience of war with a great power. Those who write in its Press, or produce the determining mass of its less ephemeral literature, are not as a rule in touch with the tragic poverty of our country and home. There is no sufficiently active sense of danger within or without for men easily to consider what the breakdown of Parliament may mean: yet that breakdown cannot but mean danger, and it is not difficult to show how near and pressing the danger may be behind the mask of content in national life and of farce in the party business.

The breakdown of any society, or of any fundamental institution in society, is but the final phase of a lingering process, the very end of which is catastrophic: so buildings collapse, so men go bankrupt, so drunkards die.

If the sense of danger were acutely present wherever decay was present, the sudden final consequences of decline might always be provided against; but it is in the very nature of decline that it should move by imperceptible steps and as it were comfortable to those who suffer it.

It should be, but it is not, a sufficient argument against anything wholly false, that falsehood, when it is erected into a system, is of its nature destructive. You cannot build upon a lie; and if the chief organ of the State attempts to build upon a lie, it should be (but for most men is not) sufficient proof that the State is thereby grievously imperilled.

In order to enforce the proof of such peril it is necessary (unfortunately) to do something more than to insist upon the general moral rottenness which public falsehood involves. It is necessary to insist upon particular examples in which direct and tangible peril to the State may be illustrated.

Five consequences of the Parliamentary rot may, among others, be chosen as the chief, and each of them can be shown to involve tangible and real peril to the nation.

(1) It puts public responsibility upon men unfitted to bear it.

(2) It defers reform in institutions and the uptaking of new weapons in defence and new methods in life at a rate progressively less than the change in the modern world around us.

(3) It permits minor legislation intensely provocative and unpopular, and therefore causative of intense and increasing friction in the public working of society.

(4) It produces, through the financial corruption of that class which not only legislates but also administrates and judges, an increasing crop of effects wasteful, impoverishing, or directly harmful to the community.

(5) Finally, it prevents the nation as a whole from ordering matters in which an active national opinion is of the first concern; to wit, defence, finance, and foreign policy.

Let us consider these five definite points of peril in detail:

(1) We say in the first place that the Party System puts public responsibility upon the shoulders of men unfitted to bear it.

It will be the tendency of all those who may be indoctrinated by the Party Press (and what other Press is there!) to doubt this truth. The politicians are so much talked of in that Press that men come to think them great and the worthy inheritors of the past. But when some heavy task is suddenly laid upon their shoulders, how contemptible is the collapse! The experiment is not often tried, and the ordeal has not often to be gone through. War is infrequent, grave public tumult more infrequent still, and of the pitiful results of our recent foreign policy the public is kept ignorant. But whenever the curtain is lifted (as it was in the beginning of the South African War, and as it has been for many "superseded" Englishmen since the close of it), the truth of what we say here is apparent.

The type of man who normally succeeds in obtaining office under the roles of the party game is not fit to administer the affairs of State.

There are, of course, elements in the position which mask this dangerous truth. For instance, the professional politician has behind him the very large and excellently trained staff of public officials which some look upon as the ultimate supplanter of the hopeless Parliamentary decline.

Again, a proportion of those who struggle for office, a small and diminishing proportion, are men of outstanding ability who have entered a political career because money prizes in such a career under our present system are so considerable; and these men, though warped by the necessities of their position, still support the falling standard of ability in the political ring.

We must also count the young men of family who are given office as of right, whose necessities of intrigue are therefore less than those of their middle class colleagues.

Nevertheless, it should be noted that the effect of the Party System on even the cleverer politicians is to reduce the normal level of their intelligence. It is quite incredible that such men as Mr Asquith and Mr Lloyd George, Mr Balfour and Mr F. E. Smith[23] could under any other circumstances give expression to such imbecilities as those which constantly adorn their public speeches. They would not talk like that at dinner or at their clubs. But the standard of intellect in politics is so low that men of moderate mental capacity have to stoop in order to reach it.

Examples of this in men who are after all highly educated, and move in a well-instructed world, will occur to everyone. They could hardly be explained in any other way than by the proportion of energy which is wasted under the Party System in bad rhetoric and worse intrigue, which are utterly useless to the Commonwealth.

We have the Prime Minister telling us that the more capital we export the better; his followers solemnly assuring us that export of capital is equivalent to an export of manufactured goods from this country—simply because they have been given orders to reiterate that absurd proposition.* We have Mr Chamberlain, some years ago, considering the Seven Years' War as the consequence and successor of the American War of Independence. We have Mr Goschen telling the House that submarines are the weapon of the weaker power, and that there is nothing odd in England's being behindhand with them. We have a parallel, many years afterwards, in Mr Haldane's provision of aviation for British forces. We have Mr Balfour telling us that Lord Milner was of a type "which only this country could produce." To the honour of the House a certain number of its Members smiled. We have Mr George proclaiming that the financial resources of this country are greater than any in the world. We have the present Minister for Education expressing astonishment (and sincerely feeling it) that the adherence of Catholics was necessary to his scheme which (but for one quarter of the population of South Lancashire) commanded a general acceptation.

Thus, also, the politicians are continually driven to make appeals on grounds which every educated man knows to be absurd, but which are thought (often falsely) to be just good enough for the multitude. Thus everybody knows that £40,000 would be a drop in the ocean in relation to the funds of our political parties—it is less than the usual price of a peerage—yet a man of the intellectual standing of Mr Balfour is induced to echo the foolish outcry about "American dollars," and to suggest that such a sum in the hands of

---

* Members particularly picked out as the "Official Economists of the team" were most ardent in this contention! It is as though a proposition in chemistry or mathematics were to be left to advocates with an axe to grind.

Mr Redmond[24] constitutes a menace to the purity of English politics. A corresponding case on the other side may be found in the attempt of Liberal politicians to suggest that in consequence of Protection all the inhabitants of the Continent of Europe live on offal,
and that the excellent black bread, which many Englishmen go to
special restaurants in London to obtain, would be refused with con-
tumely by the British Unemployed. Such suggestions could not be
put forward, in the presence of a reasonably educated public, unless
the politicians were relying upon the educated classes to connive at
the falsehood with the object of deluding the populace.

No doubt the politicians do ascribe this passion for party to
their social equals, but that is because in this, as in other matters,
they are behind the time. Probably the Press has helped to deceive
them.

But in spite of all this the truth remains that the standard
of ability, reading, and experience in political life is low, and the
continual preoccupation of the politician in petty and personal
calculations, and in the struggle to maintain his place against com-
petitors of his own kidney, leaves no sufficient margin of leisure or
of energy for any development in his character that may be useful
to the State. To these causes of failure we must of course add the
power which rich men possess of purchasing executive positions
for themselves or their relatives: a power which tends more and
more to lower the average of ability upon the two Front Benches.

(2) Next, as we have said, the system involves peril from the
tardiness which it imposes upon moral and material reform.

The policy, perhaps a necessary policy, of establishing national
granaries has not yet been so much as considered. The fortifica-
tion of our naval bases has only had questions asked upon it so far;
the Party System has not yet chosen to discuss it, and the naval
bases of this country are virtually unfortified. The same disease
has retarded any thorough remodelling of the military forces of
the country. We were for some time (and through party) badly
behindhand with submarines; we are still hopelessly behindhand
with military aviation; we have not tackled, or have only just begun to tackle, after ten years of petrol traffic, the problem of the

roads; there is no attempt as yet to co-ordinate the railway system, legislate upon rates for agricultural produce, or to subject these national bugbears to any effective form of national control–and so forth. All those things which an active and informed administration would effect by immediate decisions either do not come at all, or come after years wasted in the unfruitful play of partly opposing and partly allied party men.

Two examples of such delays pushed to the point which destroys the utility of a reform are before us.

This country, more than any other European country, had the opportunity of finding revenue from the expansion of its great towns. Provision for the taxation of ground values in those great towns, before the agricultural landlords, over whose fields the towns grew, had acquired an uninterrupted habit and a proscriptive right of complete control, would have richly endowed the State. Nothing was done until this last Budget; and what was done then comes, in the first place, too late to supply revenue on a sufficient scale, and is, in the second place, blunderingly made to apply not to areas specifically urban, but to a number of cases in which the policy produces the maximum of irritation with the minimum of revenue.

The other example is the menacingly rapid expansion of the numbers of unemployed; that is, of destitute men outside the narrow ranks of skilled and organised labour. The whole of this toppling problem has been allowed to accumulate during the present generation, and all that the Party System has managed to do–and that with the object of capturing the so-called "Labour" Party–has been the establishment of "Labour Exchanges," of which the best that can be said is that they have had no apparent effect, and the worst that they have sometimes proved useful in providing blackleg labour.

While there was a demand for land by small holders it was not met; while there was yet a chance of establishing small ownership in the English counties, no one availed himself of that chance in the political world. The party machine was otherwise employed.

(3) Next, as we have said, to this negative evil there is the positive evil that minor legislation of an intensely unpopular

character, and often of an impracticable character, passes almost without comment, because it is not made a matter for party warfare. The Crimes Prevention Act, which is certainly intolerable, and, if we may trust the declarations of the present Home Secretary, is actually breaking down, is a case in point. It was treated as "non-controversial" in the House of Commons; that is, the bosses calmly proposed to agree that a man who had poached three times upon their land, or three times "lifted" the pocket-handkerchiefs or any other trifle of the wealthier classes, should be *imprisoned for life* at the discretion of his jailers. It was only at the last moment that the discovery of this amazing proposal by a small group of private members so far modified it as to add *only five years* to the legal maximum sentence; and even in that last atrocious form the House of Commons refused to divide upon it!

The exasperating folly of such clauses (due to the fertile brain of Mr Samuel) as those which make it criminal for a boy to purchase a cigarette (unless it contain hay, or some other weed different from tobacco), and which forbid the poor to send their children for the supper beer, are other examples to the point. The tyrannic tomfoolery of the Black List, now happily dead; the cynical iniquity of the Betting Laws–statutes framed directly in the interests of the rich–and a host of others, might be cited.

In the near future, unless public opinion is sufficiently alert, Mrs Webb's amiable proposal that men found out of employment may be compelled to work in prisons–a proposal which is already said to have been agreed on as "non-controversial" by the two Front Benches, and which is gravely entertained in the Minority Report upon the Poor Law–may be law before we know it.

Now these minor things, at the best futile,* at the worst perhaps only inhuman, do not destroy a State; but an accumulation of them is an accumulation of sand in the bearings. Of late years they have accumulated very fast, and they simply could not have

---

* Every reader can suggest an addition of his own to such a list–the bullying of the publican, for instance, and the wretched nagging of the primary education system, etc.

become law if Parliament were even moderately in touch with the public opinion of the country.

(4) Our fourth point, the practical effect of the corruption of the governing class, may be briefly illustrated by the mere mention of three examples: the gross and proved scandals in connection with the South African commissariat, scandals which were admittedly but a sample of the way in which the public millions were stolen, went unpunished.

The politicians refuse to interfere with the Rockefeller Oil Trust and the low flash point upon which it insists.

Land purchase in Ireland, the one wise policy which the wretched machine has ground out in a generation, has stuck: it cannot be started again until the sham-fighters come to some sort of an agreement.

(5) Finally—and the future historian will find this by far the most important point of the whole—those matters which in every healthy state are supremely the concern of public opinion and the mass of the citizens, that is, external relations and defence, have left the sphere of Parliament.

They are said to be "above party"; and so, thank God, they are; but being above party, and therefore above the ridiculous manoeuvres of the present House of Commons, no national organ exists whereby they can be nationally handled. The grave problem of India, the position of the English "Advisors" in Egypt, our attitude towards the groups of continental powers, what army we shall have and how it shall be administered—these things are not permitted to occupy the House of Commons for more than a very few hours a year, and the debate upon them is no more than an empty show.

As the House of Commons now is, the rule is undoubtedly a wise one: better a hack at the Foreign Office, ignorant of Europe and the world, than men trained in the Party System pretending to speak of foreign affairs, let alone to direct them. Better the blundering action of a professional advocate at the India Office than dangerous protests which could never be followed by action, and that would be uttered by men in the House of Commons whose lack of position at home does not correspond to their fictitious importance in the East.

Yet what could more properly concern a true representative assembly than the establishment and preservation of English power in the great dependencies of England, and the place of England in her international relations with the continent of Europe?

There is no better proof, indeed, at once of the depths to which Parliament has sunk, and of the danger of that decline, than the firm but necessary withdrawal of such entertainment as the discussion of vital policies from the "freely chosen representatives of the nation." In the absence of the play of public opinion upon these vital policies we are compelled to take the second best, the merely personal decisions of professional politicians acting in secret; but even that has become preferable to the decision of the House of Commons in its present condition of a mere function of the "Machine."

These are the perils: they are glaring to anyone who will consider his country and its institutions, not as a remote and unchangeable body, but as one of many capable and eager rivals of whom some one or more may at any moment become an eager and capable enemy under arms. . . . Still more is it true that those who see the social condition of England as it is, and contrast it with the social condition of the countries around it, perceive how acute and immediate, though still masked, are the dangers springing from the degradation of the House of Commons. If ever there was a case for using the discredited phrase, "Something must be done," the occasion is here.

# VII

# CAN IT BE MENDED?

HEN THE QUESTION is asked: "Can a dying institution be revived?" it is in the whole tendency of modern learning to answer that it can not.

The House of Commons has ceased to be an instrument of Government. Its ancient functions have been killed under the prolonged and continuous action of hypocrisy. It affords today (if we except the three Irish parties, which have a definite political object and pursue that object) no more than an opportunity for highly lucrative careers. That career is founded upon the bamboozlement of the public (whose faculty for being duped these professionals hope to prey upon indefinitely), with the complicity of nobodies content to write MP after their name as a sufficient reward for supporting the Party System: to whom, of course, must be added the lawyers and businessmen for whom Parliament offers definite financial rewards, and that in proportion to their indifference to their representative duties.

All modern scholarship, we repeat, would tend to say of any institution which had fallen into such a condition that it was past praying for; and history is there with a hundred examples to support this modern conclusion.

We have in history case after case of a national institution falling into contempt and some other more vigorous organ supplanting it. The greatest case of all is, of course, the slow substitution of the Empire upon the ruins of the ancient Roman system of government.

It is here precisely that the crux of our problem comes in. Nothing is appearing that can take the place of Parliament. In its decay and futility it still makes our laws, and makes them and unmakes them at a greater rate than ever it did before. True, most of those laws are the work of the permanent officials; but some of them, or some parts of them, are due to the professional politicians.*

In other words, the House of Commons, though fallen into a universally recognised decay, is still our only instrument for making laws. Nothing is rising to take its place, and in its decay it continues to work very appreciable evil.

The progress of the disease is now so rapid, its probable future effect so menacing, that desperate as it must always be to attempt to revive a dying institution, it is the business of every man who cares for his country in the crisis through which it is passing to ask whether some remedy might not be devised.

Electoral changes will do nothing. A mere extension of the franchise, if the party machine were left as it is, would make little or no difference. Where today ten thousand apathetic men are seized by the paid agents of the machine and worried to the polls in groups as nearly equal as can be arranged by the managers of the show, tomorrow twenty thousand would be similarly drilled and run. The abolition of plural voting is common sense, but it would go nowhere near the root of the trouble. If it gave to one of the two teams a permanent preponderance over the other, the honour which obtains among gentlemen would compel the two in combination to devise some cry which should make the parties more nearly equal again.

To forbid canvassing would have the effect of course of enormously reducing the number of voters, the vast majority of whom vote under a sort of moral compulsion, and after several days of heavy badgering, concluded by a forced march to the polls. The bulk of men can never really care for the issues, either false or unimportant, which the bosses provide them with: nay, in the last election there was no issue at all, and the people were too weary to invent one for themselves, as they had done in the Chinese Labour Agitation in 1906.

But this decrease in the actual number of voters, though it would show up the nonsense, would have no practical effect: the

---

* Thus the land clauses in the Budget are known to be the suggestions of Sir Edward Grey, and the ill-thought-out, crude, and most unjust licensing clauses are ascribed to the Chancellor himself.

game would still be played just as it was played before, and the actors would be of the same general competence in human affairs.

Payment of election expenses and payment of members are measures obviously desirable in themselves, but they would do little to break the Party System now, though they might once have done much to prevent its coming into existence in its present form. The official expenses of an election are a very small fraction of what the candidate has to find, so that their payment by the State would still leave the independent at a grave disadvantage as compared with the party hack, who could draw without limit on the Party Funds. The payment of members might make it easier for an honest man to remain independent, but it would in no way restrain the Front Benches from corrupting members by the promise in the future of pecuniary rewards larger and of a far more stable character. To the contractor, the merchant, the newspaper owner who enters politics with an eye to their corruption, the little sum thus guaranteed is insignificant. The great press of lawyers are looking for posts, the least of which will be a matter of £800 a year, the highest of £10,000 and £15,000. The professional men, to whom this or that permanent job as an inspector or departmental chief is the bribe, would not be the less eager to take money because he had already received it.

It has been suggested that the auditing of the secret Party Funds might undermine the Party System. To inaugurate such a practice would certainly deal the Party System a heavy blow, but the success would not be final. Side by side with the officially audited Party Fund another secret fund would at once spring up. A drastic penalty might indeed be attached to any such form of secret bribery.

But the law would tend to be a dead letter in the absence of an alert public opinion behind it; for secret bribery, when it has become a national custom, is not so easy to eliminate. Nothing is less easy to prove, since all parties to the crime are concerned in defending it and in hiding it, and no one person can feel himself aggrieved. It may further be urged that the very high expenses of an election remaining what they are, the depletion of the Party Funds, which would probably follow the publication of their accounts, would advantage the wealthy candidate as against the poor one. The independent candidate would indeed benefit, for his funds would be no less than now, while those of his official opponents might probably be reduced; but the poor man financed by the Party System would probably suffer. Whether or no this would be an advantage–in other words, whether the direct rule of the rich is better or worse than the rule of their hired dependants–may be an open question. In any case, with the payment of official election expenses by the State, and the stricter limitation of unofficial expenses, this tendency might be checked.

A law which we are inclined to think would be even more to the purpose would be one whereby the duration of Parliament should be limited within a certain short fixed period (four years at the very most), and should be indissoluble within that period.

The effect of this reform, were it made law, would be immediate. A vote of censure upon the executive of the day (the King, as our forefathers called the thing) would not entail upon those who passed it the expense, disturbance, and personal peril of a general election. They would be free to vote; and the executive, that is the two Front Benches, would have to bow to their will.

The mere appearance of an adumbration of independent voting made the late Sir Henry Campbell-Bannerman and the other professional politicians give way in the matter of the Trades Disputes Bill. The principle has already entered the House of Commons, and all that is necessary is to seat it firmly by forbidding the professional politicians the right to dissolve Parliament.

In this connection it may be well to mention the suggestion made by Mr Jowett, MP,[25] in his excellent pamphlet, "What is the Use of Parliament?"* Mr Jowett would abolish the Ministry with

---

* This little pamphlet, of no more than thirty pages, should be in the hands of everyone who is interested in the present decay of Parliament, and concerned to find a remedy. The futility of the Commons procedure, the effect produced by the House of Commons on a member submitted to that procedure, has never been more lucidly or accurately put. The examples chosen are peculiarly striking and typical. The remedy Mr Jowett proposes is not only worthy of debate, but will provoke it, and there will be conflict of opinion upon it: there can be no conflict on the value, sincerity, and effect of the exposure upon which the tract is based. It is the second of the *Pass On* pamphlets, published by the

its collective responsibility altogether, and substitute a number of Departmental Committees of the House, similar to those that transact business on local councils. All parties would be represented on these, and to them the permanent officials would be responsible. The Minister would presumably be retained, but only as chairman of the Committee, where he might on any given question be outvoted by his colleagues, and the decision of the Committee might be reversed by the House. Neither of these events would, under Mr Jowett's scheme, lead to any political "crisis"; the Ministry would not resign, neither would there be any dissolution. This last condition is essential, for otherwise the Minister could always secure a majority both on the Committee and in the House by threatening resignation or dissolution; and the Party System would remain almost unaltered. If, therefore, Mr Jowett's plan is to succeed, it must be accompanied by the provision already discussed of fixing by law the duration of Parliament, and taking from the Front Benches the right of arbitrarily forcing a dissolution.

With this reservation, it may at once be allowed that Mr Jowett's scheme, if freely and honestly carried out, would not only smash the Party System, but provide a proper working machinery for a free deliberative assembly.

But, as things stand, what chance is there of honestly carrying out such a scheme, even if it could get accepted on paper?

If the Committees were packed with partisans, placemen, and place-hunters, the Minister would give them only such information as he chose, and would dictate the policy which they would obediently endorse. The Committees might even be used to increase (if that be possible) the modern irresponsibility of members, by affording a buffer between them and the House. As to independent members, it would be easy to keep them off Committees, or at any rate off the particular Committees where they might be dangerous. Mr Victor Grayson has told the world how he applied

Clarion Press, of 44 Worship St., E.C., and may be purchased for a penny, or by post 1½d.

to be put on a Committee of Social Reform, and was immediately told that he had been appointed to sit on the Committee to consider the *Irish Linen Marks Bill* !

That is perhaps no insignificant indication of what might happen if Mr Jowett's plan were adopted in a House still dominated by the Party System.

The institution of primaries and the choice of candidates by their localities would be valuable enough; but it must be remembered that it will be no easy task to graft primaries with their postulate of popular initiative on to English society, as it is at present.

Another suggestion made for the democratisation of our politics is the Referendum. This proposal, excellent in itself, has of late been rendered a trifle ridiculous by its sudden and obviously insincere exploitation by one of the party teams. Mr Balfour's "Referendum," so far as its nature can be guessed at, amounts to no more than that the "bosses" of the two sides acting, as always, in collusion, should from time to time entertain the people by submitting to their judgment proposals in which they take no interest whatsoever, a course which might also prove convenient as a means of burying some highly unpopular proposal insisted on by a wealthy subscriber or a too persistent colleague. The only Referendum which will prove of the slightest value to the people will be the Referendum accompanied by the Initiative; in other words, the right of the people (as expressed by a certain number of electors) to determine on what subjects they shall vote. Such a right would indeed be of incalculable value; but before it is likely to be obtained the people must develop a sufficiently alert political sense to make their initiative a reality.

It would seem, then, that changes in political machinery will prove either impossible or ineffective, unless the people can be awakened to political consciousness and to a resolution to make their will prevail. An alert democracy, even with unchanged machinery, could knock the bottom out of the Party System tomorrow by refusing to elect party hacks and by sending to Parliament men fully determined to make an end of the corruption and unreality of our politics. In proportion as the mass of men understand the nature of the present system, and resolve to replace it by a better, the Party System will become more and more difficult to work.

The political education of the democracy is therefore the first step towards a reform.

The first need is exposure. To tell a particular truth with regard to a particular piece of corruption is of course dangerous in the extreme; the rash man who might be tempted to employ this weapon would find himself bankrupted or in prison, and probably both. But the general nature of the unpleasant thing can be drilled into the public by books, articles, and speeches. True, the Press will do its utmost to prevent the dissemination of the truth with regard to public life; for the Press, as we have seen, is one of the chief accomplices in this side of the national decline. But it is an error to imagine that publicity, because it is at first restricted, will be ineffectual.

So suspicious is an increasing section of the public growing of the whole political scheme, and of the printed support of it, that the continued exposure of the evil, even if it be undertaken by comparatively few men, has a wide effect.

It may have for its organs of expression only a few and ill-capitalised papers; but one man speaks to another, and truth has this particular quality about it (which the modern defenders of falsehood seem to have forgotten), that when it has been so much as suggested, it of its own self and by example tends to turn that suggestion into a conviction.

You say to some worthy provincial, "English Prime Ministers sell peerages and places on the Front Bench."

He is startled, and he disbelieves you; but when a few days afterwards he reads in his newspaper of how some howling nonentity has just been made a peer, or a member of the Government, the incredible sentence he has heard recurs to him. When in the course of the next twelve months five or six other nonentities have enjoyed this sort of promotion (one of whom perhaps he may know from other sources than the Press to be a wealthy man who uses his wealth in bribery) his doubt grows into conviction.

That is the way truth spreads, and that, by the way, was why this book was written.

The truth, when it is spoken for some useful purpose, must necessarily seem obscure, extravagant, or merely false; for, were it of common knowledge, it would not be worth expressing. And truth being fact, and therefore hard, must irritate and wound; but it has that power of growth and creation peculiar to itself which always makes it worth the telling.

Again, exposure (within the limits which the machine is compelled to allow—and the machine is not without its power over the judiciary) works in a manner less just, but still of some value; it works by ridicule.

Men love to laugh, and if you can present your liar, your coward, your place-hunter, your hypocrite, not as hypocrite, place-hunter, coward, and liar, but as a buffoon, though the action may be unjust, you have not done wholly ill. As a buffoon he is well advertised; once advertised, a discovery of all that he really is will follow.

The Party System is not principally, though it is largely, a piece of buffoonery; principally it is hypocritical; it reposes upon falsehood; it has for its main instruments avarice and fear.

These things are dreadful, not ridiculous; but their ridiculous side can be happily harped upon until men attend: comprehension of the rest will follow.

For instance, during the late election one of the younger men who had just been put upon the Front Bench by the machine said that the "gulf" between the two Front Benches was "unbridgeable"; he said it to a mass of men much poorer than himself, whose votes make him what he is. *They* had no opportunity to see behind what scenes the actor moves. He deliberately deceived them. Well, this young man had his place from marrying a lady whose uncle had made many thousands in one half of the team; the same lady had a first cousin who had made a much larger number of thousands in the other half of the team. One of these new-found relatives was labelled "Opposition," the other "Government," and the poor men who listened were told that there was an "unbridgeable gulf" between the one relative and the other!

It would be well if the world were such that falsehood of this sort could be burnt out. Failing that, to make it ridiculous is no small advance to its removal.

After exposure the second line of attack is the advocacy of definite reform *within the machine itself.* By which we do not mean a change in the procedure of Parliament, for, in the first place, Parliament is free to effect that whenever it chooses, and, in the second place, it is so hopelessly corrupt that it will not of itself ever effect the manifold and detailed reforms which would be necessary for its purification.

But it might be possible, by scattering and using a sufficient number of trained workers, to extract from candidates definite pledges during the electoral period, which would have an effect upon the Party System comparable to the introduction of wedges into the diseased fabric of an ancient tree. Of the method of action of these pledges we will speak in a moment; for it is notorious that as things now are, the pledges of a candidate are worth nothing, if only for the simple reason that no candidate has any initiative, let alone the innumerable other reasons, one of which is that very few candidates under the present system have either any intention of carrying out their pledges or take any steps towards that end.

The principal pledge which should and could be extracted from candidates would be a pledge that they would vote against the Government—whatever its composition—unless there were carried through the House of Commons, within a set time, those measures to which they stood pledged already in their election addresses and on the platform. A schedule could easily be drawn up, within whose limits certain measures were required by the electorate to pass the House of Commons.

A supreme advantage attaches to this method, and a grave weakness.

We will deal with the advantage first. The supreme advantage is that by this method even the professional politician cannot wriggle.

Thus, in the matter of Chinese labour it was easy to pledge a man "to vote that the Chinese should leave South Africa"; but had he publicly promised to vote against the Government unless the first cargo of them had left South Africa before the 1$^{st}$ of March 1906, and to vote against them again *upon all measures they might propose* after the 31$^{st}$ of December 1906, if by that time the last Chinaman had not left, your politician would have been caught. He could not get out of it by saying that "his vote would have involved the fall of the Government, with all its rich promise of democratic legislation, etc., etc." The pledge would stand.

Such a pledge for definite action would be efficacious—which no pledge now is. It would hold up the party boss and say, "Here are you and yours with such and such salaries. You can bend to the popular will, or you can go." By such a pledge, and by such a pledge alone, could short parliaments and the withdrawal of the professionals' power to dissolve Parliament be obtained.

In a word, a rigid pledge of this sort is a real instrument of war, or, to use the more accurate metaphor, of surgery. With it one might cut out the cancer.

Now for the weakness of the method:

That weakness does not consist (as we may imagine the professional politician at once remarking) in the fact that anyone might ask for any pledge, and that a mere confusion would arise.

The people know very well what they want, and they want a very few and definite things; and it is precisely in those things, as they are wanted with each phase of the national life, that the politicians cheat and betray the people.

For instance, the Trades Disputes Bill and Chinese Labour are excellent examples of what we mean.

Moreover, if (as will probably be the case) a multitude of pledges might be demanded, that or those which had a definite popular demand behind them would very quickly be appreciated in public meetings. Cut off as the politician is from the life of England, the insistent presentation of one type of question throughout the election would get to him at last, and he would be afraid of it. But above all things it will be essential that the questioner should ask him not to "pledge" himself in general—a practice of which everyone is by this time heartily sick, for it is futile—but to pledge himself in particular that if the thing were not passed within a definite date (by the House of Commons, not by the Lords of the Crown), then he would vote against the Government upon all measures whatsoever.

No, the real weakness of the proposition lies in this: that the mass of men have so despaired of the House of Commons and its methods that no sufficient organisation with this end could be constructed. What they feel is: "The old thing is fading; let it fade. The enormous effort required for making any impression on it at all is not worth while."

Well, if it so prove, if freemen will not make an effort to control their representatives, then it is necessary to decide that the law-making institution of England, which has already ceased to be an instrument of Government, is done with.

A spasmodic life may be, and probably will be, lent it in the desperate attempt of the professionals to keep up the old interest in their trade. Questions of real import may be raised. It is conceivable, for instance, that a "Conservative" leader might frankly adopt Protection, or a "Liberal" prefer Adult Suffrage. It is exceedingly likely, nay almost certain, that, as matter of self-preservation, the politicians of the immediate future will establish temporary divisions upon which true interests can range themselves; but they will not thus restore Parliament, for purpose is lacking to them. The body will jerk, perhaps—it will not revive.

For on this thing all observant men are now settled: the House of Commons in its present inaptitude, producing as "leaders" the type of men who play at the rotation of the party game, cannot deal with the vast and rapidly changing necessities of the country at home, where men starve—or abroad, where (behind their backs) they are humbled.

The degraded Parliament may ultimately be replaced by some other organ; but no such other organ appears to be forming, and until we get our first glimpse of it we are in for one of those evil spaces, subject to foreign insult and domestic misfortune, which invariably attach to nations when, for a period, they lose grip over their own destinies.

# A NOTE ON CO-OPTION

N CONNECTION with this system of choosing the chief officers of the State, it will be of advantage to pause a moment and consider fully its modern meaning. An evil may often be perfectly well known to exist, and may even have become a commonplace, and yet not be realised. It may be all the less realised, and the conception of it may be all the fainter in the public mind, precisely because it *has* come to be taken for granted and has become a commonplace. Let us first, therefore, repeat clearly what the process of selection is as compared with that of our great rivals.

In the German Empire the men ultimately responsible for the chief posts of administration are chosen by one man of known character with definite duties attached to his office and under no necessity for intrigue among equals, or for the deception of inferiors. That man is the Emperor; his judgment, being a personal judgment, may be wise or unwise, but it is exercised for public ends and in the public view, and, precisely because it is personal, is subject to public appreciation. It is on this very account that the various men successively picked out in our generation to be responsible for military, naval, and civil matters, stand out as prominent and great; or, again, recede as small and incompetent, and are judged, as it were, upon a certain scale of merit, because their merits and aptitudes are not fictions but realities; they are really chosen for a real work for which they are supposed, rightly or wrongly, to be really apt. And if they fail it is the failure of judgment in those who choose, not a failure of motive.

In the French Republic a method superior from the point of view of democratic theory, inferior in continuity and personal initiative, exists. Ministries are formed in any one of an almost indefinite number of combinations, the object of the one last arranged being to secure the support of a majority in Parliament: and as that majority is, in spite of much corruption and many contemptible features in French Parliamentary life, at least independent of any such self-appointed organisation as "the two Front Benches," it fluctuates at will; in other words, unless those men are chosen who, each in his own department, can satisfy a majority of the Chamber, the Ministry will be rejected. Sometimes the Ministry will fall as a whole and be replaced by another combination more nearly representing the tone of Parliament at the moment; sometimes members of it prove worthless or unworthy, are dispensed with, and the Ministry is "reconstructed"; but the Ministry must always be representative of a real majority in the Commons, or it is not allowed to administrate, and this is true of each of its important appointments singly as well as of the Cabinet as a whole. There is no machinery for compelling Parliament to accept whatever it may be given in the way of Ministers under pain of dissolution and a general election. Still less is there a permanent understanding between the Radical group and the Conservative group, or their chief men, by which automatic voting can be secured in favour of any combinations "passed and approved" by those chief men behind the scenes.

In the United States of America, where Federal responsibility, though its initiative is of capital importance, covets a more restricted area than the responsibility of British Ministers, it is, as in Germany, the direct and responsible will of one man which is mainly responsible for the choice of the heads of departments, and these are particularly excluded from the action of the Party System, which is almost as rigid as our own. True, that "monarch" is elected upon a party ticket, but it is characteristic of this wise provision for the selection of a single man to exercise ultimate authority at the head of the State, that his personality is ever a capital feature. In proceeding to a Presidential election great National Conventions have the chief influence and weight. Not always, but usually, a real leader emerges from what is not only a real but sometimes a frenzied competition, and one has only to cite the names of the American Presidents to see how large a proportion of them are the names of men who, whether we approve them or disapprove them, acted, led, and did with the objects of the Commonwealth before their eyes. In less than thirty names you may count Washington and Jefferson, Van Buren, the elder Harrison, Lincoln, Grant, Cleveland, and Roosevelt, and these are but the most prominent of all.

Now what happens here?

We are not asking what *did* happen, when, with the machinery apparently similar to our own today, very different results were obtained. We are asking what *does* happen as a fact at the present moment.

What happens is this: an existing set of persons, a dozen or so, distributed between the two Front Benches, exercise the right to recruit their permanent organisation, to recruit it gradually and to recruit it continuously. Over this right Parliament has no actual check. The Crown is reported, once or twice at the most in a whole lifetime, to have some modifying influence in the case of a couple or at most three selections. How far the rumour is true we cannot tell, because the whole process is conducted with that secrecy which has become the rule of our political life. This clique, perpetually recruiting itself by co-option, has become a definite organism separate from the rest of the political body, with the inevitable result that, as we have seen, and as we have insisted upon throughout this book, it has become more and more a family affair, introduction to which is mainly secured by personal and private influence.

Some will argue that a proportion of the men so chosen are and will continue to be of service to the Commonwealth and of ability. That is true – and the flaw in the argument is that it would be equally true under any system of government whatsoever, however corrupt and however self-seeking. The decencies must be maintained, and a certain minimum of efficiency is as necessary to the conduct of this arbitrary form as of any other arbitrary form of government; but it is as true of this arbitrary form as of other arbitrary forms, that they tend to become inefficient in proportion as they escape from public control and public criticism, and the most sanguine can hardly believe that, by a pure coincidence, a little group of men so closely interrelated must continuously and traditionally form the best or even a good selection of public officers.

But (another will object) this same machinery existed in the past, and gave results under which Great Britain continually increased in prosperity and power. This is true; but there were three elements present in the past which have gradually lost effect and are now eliminated: the first was aristocracy, which, whether we approve it or disapprove it, has always had certain characteristics wherever it has existed in a State, among which was the spontaneous selection of a sufficient number of men within its ranks who should properly conduct the common weal. An aristocracy admittedly in power has, in its effects, something of the representative character which a national monarchy possesses; and, what is more, selection being frankly confined to a certain and fairly large area in which is to be discovered one type of man, there is an active and real competition within that area.

Secondly, the Crown possessed a real determining influence which watched over each Ministry and clearly affected it.

Thirdly, and much the most important, there was the real and effective control of Parliament.

Today all those three salutary factors are gone.

It is true, of course, that there are remains of aristocratic tradition, but they are not dominant. They work only where aristocracy is combined with great wealth, and they prefer great wealth to lineage. Now, it is in the essence of the healthy working of aristocratic institutions that they shall be open, national, and admitted: when they work under tolerance, as it were, and with dwindling effect, their function in the Commonwealth is petty and directly evil.

The influence of the Crown may revive. It is a part of the game the self-appointed clique play today to hint mysteriously from time to time at the existence or revival of that power, but it is not definite, and it is certainly exceedingly weak—if it exists at all. The public knows nothing of it; and if the hints dropped by the professional politicians are as truthful in this connection as their statements upon any other matter, they may be safely neglected.

As for the control of Parliament, by far the chief factor, it has utterly disappeared. It is impossible to conceive of any appointment made to either Front Bench, however monstrous or absurd, which would lead to remonstrance from the drilled voting machine which the Front Benches control; nor can any critic of what we here advance point out such remonstrance during the course of many years.

To sum up, the method of recruitment is simply that against which every corporate body particularly and specially guards itself. It is an understood matter, wherever men act in common, in a college, a public company, or any other form of activity, their Executive must be watched, chosen, and controlled; and that the one disease most fatal to the success and health of the whole is the letting of the Executive become a clique which has and exercises the power of appointing friends and relatives in its own renewal. Yet that is exactly what the Executive in the most important corporate body of all has become. The Executive of Parliament is a clique, possessing and using the power to renew itself by the co-option of relatives, connections, and friends; and this method, with just so many exceptions as may keep the system alive, is the normal and recognised method by which we have come to choose those who shall be responsible for the national safety and well-being when next some peril shall arise.

# A NOTE ON COLLUSION

IT IS EXCEEDINGLY IMPORTANT in this connection to observe a due proportion of criticism. That which is concealed, and that the true nature of which is carefully and deliberately misrepresented to the public, cannot be exposed by a mere negation of the public's false conception. For, in the first place, no such general conception would be held by a great number of men were there not an element of truth in it; and, in the second place, all false intrigue designed to deceive great bodies of men is necessarily careful and tentative in its action.

When, therefore, insistence is laid on the collusion maintained between the leaders of either nominal "side" in the House of Commons, it is not and cannot be meant, by their most ardent critics, that there is neither ground of opposition between them, nor even that collusion is their chief preoccupation. The process may be best compared to one of those active but ordered struggles wherein men find so much of their occupation and even profit: ranging from a game of cards at the least to the great competitive activities of commerce at the greatest.

Now in all such engagements the interest of the sport and (if there is money in it) the avidity for gain bring out real differences of action, real conflicts of object, and even sometimes, and in proportion to the magnitude and sincerity of the affair, real passions.

Were party ever so fictitious, some elements of conflict would still remain. Had all political ideals disappeared in the business, something would have to be invented to play for. But, conversely, were party ever so real or ever so deadly earnest, something would still have to be held in common, which is the security and well-being and order of the community. Thus in the fierce competition of the great capitalists, one thing is still more important than success in the competition, and that is the maintenance by law and armed force of the whole capitalistic system. Thus also, at the other end of the scale, when men play golf or whist or bridge, one thing is more important than winning, and that is seeing that the rules shall be observed, in other words, that the game shall continue to exist and be possible.

It must therefore be granted that though the very maximum of difference were present between true and vivid political ideals, separately held and cherished by the leaders of the two parties, yet for the very existence of government by debate one thing would remain more important than those ideals, namely, the preservation of the system under which they could be discussed, and the decisions of majorities arrived at and upheld. To deny this is to admit what none can admit, save in the rarest and most absolute of conflicts, the need of civil war.

We may imagine, therefore, one leader and his followers, sincerely convinced that a war was morally justifiable, and (what is almost the same thing) of advantage to England; his opponent and his opponent's followers, as strongly convinced that it was a crime and a national disaster, and yet both those men preserving the decencies of the debate, occasionally conferring upon matters whereon the whole nation was agreed and in which administrative skill was required. We may imagine them using their efforts to keep the House of Commons united after a great defeat in a plan for recovering the national honour; that would not be collusion, that would not afford matter for criticism in the judgment of any but a fanatic.

But as things now stand, the line is drawn at an indefinite distance from this ideal line. The thing which the nominal opponents find it essential to preserve by their secret understanding, is not the security of the country nor even the order of debate, but the conditions under which they and their clique shall retain the opportunities for large salaries within and without the country, and for power. The things on which they prevent division are precisely the things on which opinion is really divided and the policy of the majority is expected to rule. The things which they forbid to arise in debate are precisely those things which form the secret basis of their position, the sale of honours and legislative power, the connection between nominal antagonists, the reform of the procedure of the House, the widening of opportunities for private members, the lowering of salaries, the establishment of control by public committees, and so forth. It is true to say that no one important policy for now fifteen years has been allowed by the two Front Benches to form a clear division in the House of Commons, with the exception of the policy of Women's Suffrage; and even in this case it lies entirely with the two Front Benches whether that policy, no matter by what majority it may be passed, is to have an opportunity of becoming law, or even of reaching Committee stage.*

The collusion we speak of is particularly apparent in matters of administration which today, in the complexity of public affairs, are of particular importance. It is strikingly apparent where the interests of great financiers are concerned: the Ministerialist who most loudly denounces the power of the rich is seeing to it that a stroke of financial policy carried on by some cosmopolitan banker in Egypt or Ceylon should be kept from the public, and his "opponent" is told of the matter, consulted upon it, and heartily supports it.

All evils tend to reach their remedy by excess, and this evil has certainly come to a pitch which should bring it very near the breaking point. If by some accident leaders have not been able to meet so as to arrange a common policy, a note will be tossed across the table at the House of Commons. Time and again the Whips confer openly to prevent a majority decision upon some matter which keenly divides opinion among rank and file. The common decision to exclude amendments to the Address which are not "official" is

---

* Thus in the form of an extension of the suffrage to the well-to-do, the two Front Benches are on the whole, or at least by a majority, agreed, and the adherence of the Labour Party to this scheme is particularly significant, for their attitude is always an index of the official view held on either side of the Speaker's chair. The alternative proposal to extend the suffrage to all women is, on the contrary, discountenanced by the two Front Benches. Time would be required to make such a scheme fit in with the machines that feed and support them.

no longer secretly negotiated, but part of the open business of the House. When new salaried posts are created, the Chancellor of the Exchequer, or whoever else is the responsible Minister in connection with it, will announce his intention of conveying the favoured names to the Front Bench he faces, and will ignore all criticism or questioning from "his own side."

In fine, it is this basis of collusion, now firmly laid down as the foundation of the whole system, which directly creates what is otherwise inexplicable and what the plain elector marvels at; to wit, the way in which even a real question, once started, at once becomes a false issue and is argued upon premises that neither interest the public nor really concern the vital points of the debate.

Thus it is proposed to increase the salary of one of the clique from £40 to £100 a week; probably the "other half" will hold their tongues–for the money is always in prospect for them later on; but if they argue it they will argue that the office is not "of a dignity" to carry such a salary! As though in this country the dignity of position corresponded with its emolument! Or, again, it is proposed to pay members of Parliament, whereupon an exceedingly wealthy Front Bench man, who has already lifted thousands out of the taxes, will jump up to suggest that the proposition is all very well for those who cannot afford to sit at Westminster, but is in danger of creating "the professional politician."

Another gentleman in a happy and irresponsible moment proposes the referendum. His "side" all suddenly cry out in chorus (only for a few days it is true) that the referendum is good because it is cheap, clear, and would avoid the turmoil coincident with an election. At once the professionals of the "other side" argue that men voting yes or no on the Licensing Bill, for instance, would not know their own minds, and that the very spirit of democracy requires that a small co-opted clique should govern the country. Nay, the crushing argument is discovered that the word referendum is not of Anglo-Saxon origin, whereupon the original defenders on the first "side" triumphantly substitute the word "poll"; and win.

This done, both parties abandon all mention of the referendum for ever.

# A NOTE ON THE PRESS

I N CONSIDERING both the evils produced by the Party System and the chance of remedying them, a reader acquainted with English life will at once be met by one of the most important factors in that life: the influence of the daily Press.

In some ways that influence is peculiar to this country; but a statement of its characteristics – the predominance of a very few great daily newspapers, the urban life in which alone the mere suggestion which they represent could have such power, the immense sums necessary to found and to conduct one, the anonymity of the opinions and information they impose and convey – all these are matters so familiar to an English reader that they may be taken for granted.

The Press is certainly devoted to the Party System: more devoted to it than is any part of the State, except the professional politicians themselves. If, then, the Press can be shown to suffer from the pressure of party-machinery, that is, if the party agents actively taint public information, then certainly we have here one of the most evil examples of its influence, and an evil that will be best corrected by the correction of its cause, the Party System itself.

If, on the contrary, the motive force is the other way, if the Press is a voluntary agent freely supporting the Party System and its hypocrisies, then in considering this poison in the source of public information we must attack not the Party System in its connection with the Press, but the Press in its connection with the Party System.

Let us examine the problem.

That the Press is grossly and even ludicrously warped in its connection with our modern machine-made politics no one will deny. The great daily papers are advocates for the one team and the other, and, in connection with political discussion, they never rise above, nor are more intelligent or lively than, mere advocacy. The policy adopted by the so-called "Liberal" team will be enthusiastically defended in the *Star,* the *Daily News,* the *Manchester Guardian,* the *Westminster Gazette,* etc. The policy put forward by the "other"* team will be similarly championed by the *Times,* the *Daily Tele-graph,* the *Birmingham Daily Post,* the *Pall Mall Gazette,* and so forth. That is a commonplace: and the superficial observer might be tempted to the conclusion—a foreigner would certainly be tempted to it—that the professional politicians were controlling the Press even more thoroughly than they control their hack followers, and presumably controlling it by the same corrupt methods.

In other words, a first approach to the problem would make us conclude that the Party System was the cause, and the warping of the Press (that is of public information) the effect. Many a man has smiled during the last few weeks to read, in the so-called "Liberal" papers, enthusiastic battle-cries, such as that the "Peers" were opposed to the "People" in the farcical election of last December. Many a man has smiled to read in "Conservative" newspapers majestic eulogies of such few commonplace and second-rate professionals as were shouting in one breath the necessity of defending the ancient Constitution of the country, and the necessity of utterly transforming one of the estates of the realm.

The absurdity of the sorry business is apparent to most readers, but it is particularly apparent to that large class of readers who know how a great newspaper is produced. Who know, for instance, that the writers on such and such a "Conservative" paper are largely Socialist; the chief influence in such another "Free Trade" paper is that of a convinced Protectionist; that the ownership of such and such an organ is divided between men who vaguely profess adherence to both teams, or, as is more common, are indifferent to the success of either.

Knowing such things, one might be tempted to say that they were the product of methods directly corrupt, such as are the familiar and common instruments of the professional politicians.

Now, as a matter of fact, they are not the results of such methods. The pressure of the politicians upon the papers can be exerted only in one form, which is the granting of honours to such of their proprietors as desire those distinctions. That is not a very powerful

---

* Just now it has no fixed name. Shall we call it (in January 1911) "Conservative"?

lever; and, as a matter of fact, it has become rather a matter of routine that such honours should be granted when they are asked for.

For instance, A, B, and C on the Treasury Bench promote a Bill for the nationalisation of a railway. They have the intention, of course, of paying the shareholders (to many of whom they are related) more than it is worth. D, E, and F (cousins, uncles, stepsons, etc. of A, B, and C) formally oppose the Bill, the success of which they ardently desire, and the financial proceeds from which they and their relatives are expecting as eagerly as any.

Mr Muggs owns a newspaper which has been supporting A, B, and C, or perhaps buys it; it continues to support A, B, and C. His brother, Johnnie Muggs, owns an opposition paper, and supports D, E, and F. When the time has come for the two teams to arrange an election and to have "a swing of the pendulum," that is to swop salaries, Mr Muggs is given his baronetcy or whatnot (no money passes in such cases); and when D, E, and F come in after the election, Johnnie Muggs, within a decent interval, gets the little handle to his name, whatever it may be.

The whole thing is native to the atmosphere of modern politics, and much less corrupt than most features of political life. It would be easy to name half a dozen great owners of newspapers who could perfectly well obtain such honours if they desired them, and who have either refused them or shown no sort of inclination for them. As for places, direct payments, jobs, contracts, and the rest, the Press is, of all the industries in the country, the least touched by the party disease where they are concerned. It would probably be impossible to point to a single case in which the support given by a newspaper to a professional politician could be connected with any money reward of the kind.

Where, then, does the cause lie? What is the motive which makes a man, otherwise honest, and one whose main duty it is to earn his living by conveying true information, talk of the "magnetic personality" of the late Sir Henry Campbell-Bannerman or the "arresting eloquence" of some member of the Churchill or Cecil families?

Primarily, it is the fact that the public, which buys the newspaper, is, by what is now a hard and fossilised journalistic tradition, supposed to desire this sort of farce. There are, of course, great numbers of the middle class, especially in the provinces, who do actually desire to have the game played in this fashion for them in the sheets which they daily read; and though half a dozen independent and instructive newspapers should arise tomorrow, fully capitalised, well advertised, and properly written, yet the mere momentum of custom would cause party to linger in the great body of the Press for many years. It would linger, we may be sure, even though the Party System itself should have disappeared: for instance, traces of it would remain for an appreciable time under the government of an open coalition.

We must take it, then, that the motive of action here is a social force not yet spent, and one which will probably outlive the Party System itself. Something of the sort is to be seen in the matter of religious and historical conventions: the Press feels itself bound to repeat these conventions long after they have ceased to have reality in the minds of its readers; and its readers, on their side, *expect* this ritual to be performed.

Against a force of this kind there is no immediate remedy. Ridicule, exposure, continual criticism, may rapidly undermine the Party System in action, and may so scatter sand into the bearings of that "machine for grinding wind" that it shall be brought to a standstill. But ridicule, exposure, and the rest will find nothing tangible to work on in the party attitude of the Press, for the simple reason that that attitude is not corrupt, but merely conventional. You can, by the habit of repeated exposure of similar jobs in the past, make a particular professional politician afraid of perpetrating some particular job in the present; and when you have made an appreciable number of the politicians afraid to act corruptly on an appreciable number of occasions, the Party System will be done for. But in the case of the Press there is nothing to expose. Its attitude is not wicked, it is merely stupid.

The true tactic of those who regret the extension of this disease to the newspapers is to continue their attack upon that Parliamentary game which is not the *cause* but which is the *object* of the newspapers' fatuity. If that game can be slackened down, put off, confused, and so ended, the Press will be ultimately the wholesomer for the change, and will lie less; but its health must come directly; no medicine will reach it till the party politician (who is the stock-in-trade of the Press) is made impossible.

Meanwhile it is difficult to see why some man of wealth and enterprise (or some group of men possessed of both these valuable but incongruous qualities) should not start a journal, the object of which should be the conveyance of information rather than the wearisome advocacy of set policies designed in conclave by the "Government" and "Opposition" Benches.

Why should it not be possible for a newspaper to lay before its readers the advantages and disadvantages of a duty on hops, while at the same time giving its readers full information upon the effect of a duty on wheat at five shillings a quarter? Why should its writers not determine against the second and in favour of the first innovation? More important still: why should we not have a stray journal or two which would print what "party" now prevents *either* "side" of journalism from printing? For instance, why should we not have journals prepared to denounce the sale of legislative power by *either* team or a corrupt job, whether of the Minister for the Fine Arts, or of his wife's cousin, the late "Opposition" Minister of Public Worship and Justice? Why should not a newspaper which thought it just to lay an increment tax upon urban land, and asinine to distribute broadcast such a farrago of details and often unanswerable questions as Form Four, express both opinions? They are not logically disconnected!

A journal which thought it necessary to increase the strength of the British Navy in capital ships need not, one would imagine, be bound to hold up Belfast as a model for the rest of Ireland; nor need a paper whose proprietor or staff thought the present expenditure upon the Navy excessive be compelled to regard the drinking of a glass of beer as an enormity.

Most men sunk in the managerial routine of journalism would say there was "no room" for such a paper, "no public" for it, and nothing but financial disaster in front of it.

Those who argue thus can never have noticed how many thousands are daily driven to consult the organs of both the nominal "sides" in order to guess at the truth which an independent journal would have given them without such labour.

There is a public of many, many thousands, especially in London, awaiting such an experiment, and it is noticeable that the best edited of the morning papers, the *Daily Mail*, continually admits discussion and adverse opinion upon matters in which the public judgment requires rather information and the balance of opinions than advocacy.

However, a pursuit of this consideration would lead us far from the object of our book, and this short section is no more than what we have called it, a "Note."

It is enough to conclude that no direct remedy is applicable to the existing Party Press: it must drag its weary way a little longer, and continue for a few more years to tell us of the dreadful antagonisms which separate the Siamese Twins of politics.

No policy is possible to the reformer save that of disregarding the official Press, of leaving it on one side, and of advancing upon the only active force remaining to the Party System, the cupidity and intrigues of those few whom it benefits. The Press has long ceased to affect opinion.*

---

* It has ceased, that is, to affect opinion where "Party" is concerned: largely because very little true opinion in the matter of party now exists. It has not, of course, ceased to affect opinion in another sense; it can affect the public very deeply indeed by its choice of information upon foreign affairs. The attempt, however, to influence the party game through the purchase of newspapers has latterly proved financially so disastrous that we shall probably not see it repeated.

# NOTES

1. Bethnal Green is a district in the east end of London, England.

2. Herbert Henry Asquith (1852–1928) was a lawyer who became Liberal MP for East Fife in 1886. He joined Gladstone's Cabinet in 1892 as Home Secretary, became Chancellor in 1906 under Campbell-Bannerman, and succeeded the latter as Prime Minister in 1908. He brought in the Old Age Pensions Act and the People's Budget, which led to "conflict" with the Tory-dominated House of Lords. The result was the forcing through of the 1911 Parliament Act which greatly restricted the powers of the Lords. Asquith effectively came to grief when thanks to the influence of Lord Northcliffe's papers – *The Daily Mail* and *The Times* – Asquith's Chancellor, David Lloyd George, was induced go into alliance with the Conservatives.

3. William Ewart Gladstone (1809–1898) entered Parliament in 1832 as a Conservative and joined the Ministry of Sir Robert Peel in 1834. There he exercised various powers at the Treasury and the Board of Trade. In 1847, he joined Lord Aberdeen's coalition government and rose to Chancellor of the Exchequer and remained in the post even when Lord Palmerston came to power a decade later. He later switched his allegiance to the Liberal Party and rapidly became its leader. In 1868 he became Prime Minister and sought, amongst other things, to get a vapid Irish Home Rule Bill through Parliament though without success. He was noted in his lifetime for his devotion to "saving" prostitutes, and recent researchers conclude that his motives were not wholly altruistic. A model Parliamentarian!

4. The London Boat Race became a national tradition when a Cambridge University student challenged a friend at Oxford University to a race in 1829. The first race was held at Henley-on-Thames, Oxfordshire but the large crowds necessitated an immediate change to Westminster. By 1845 the crowds had become so unwieldy that the race was switched to the present Putney–Mortlake location. The race takes place normally on the last Saturday of March or first Saturday in April, though of late Sunday has become popular. The course is four miles long and regularly attracts 250,000 spectators.

5. The Jameson Raid took place on December 29th, 1895 and was led by Dr. Leander Starr Jameson (1853–1917). A close friend of the British imperialist, Cecil Rhodes, he led a so-called "reform" movement which sought to allow "uitlanders" – "foreigners" in Afrikaans – to take part in the political process in

the Transvaal Boer Republic under President Paul Kruger. The real motivation for this desired political reform was the fact that gold had been discovered at Witwatersrand in the Transvaal in 1886. Needless to say, the Boers were having none of this, knowing that the "uitlanders" were a gang of greedy Britons and Jews. In his book, *The Boer War*, published by Random House, Thomas Pakenham revealed a conspiracy of British colonial officials and financiers to plunge South Africa into war. The plan was to destroy the Boer Republics, and incorporate them – and their wealth – into the British Empire. One might see it as an early example of today's "resources wars." The front man for the whole affair was Cecil Rhodes, who ensured that Jameson was supplied with 500 men and £200,000 in money (a sum of millions in today's values). Nevertheless, the Raid was botched and the Boers forced Jameson to surrender at Doornkop on January 2nd, 1896. The people behind Rhodes were Alfred Beit of Wernher, Beit & Co., the most powerful financial house in South Africa – and one linked to the Rothschild Dresdener Bank – and Lionel Phillips. The latter, along with Beit, controlled the largest mining syndicate in the country, H. Eckstein & Co. Beit's and Phillips's idea of "political participation" in the Transvaal was to try and induce "a change of direction" through the use of massive bribery. In spite of the blood on his hands and the practice of corruption, Phillips returned to England after the fall-out of the Boer War, was knighted for "services rendered," and given high position in the British Ministry of Munitions during WWI. It was knowledge of this and other shenanigans that persuaded Chesterton, Belloc and all decent English people to support the Boers against their own government – a government that actively planned war for material and political ends using people of dubious integrity.

6. Arthur James Balfour (1848–1930) entered Parliament in 1874 as a Conservative MP, and became Private Secretary to Lord Salisbury (his uncle) in 1878. He became Secretary for Scotland in 1886 and the Chief Secretary for Ireland the following year. In Ireland his anti-Irish bias and ruthlessness earned him the name "Bloody Balfour." He was Prime Minister from 1902 to 1905, and then became Foreign Secretary under Lloyd George in 1916. His lasting, bloody legacy was the "Balfour Declaration" issued in 1917 in a letter to Lord Rothschild where he proposed to establish "a national home" for Jews on land continuously occupied by Palestinians for 1,700 years. He was made an Earl in 1922.

7. William Pitt the Younger (1759–1806) was so designated in order to distinguish him from his father, William Pitt the Elder, the Earl of Chatham. Entered Parliament in 1781, becoming Chancellor of the Exchequer in the Earl of Shelburne's administration the following year. However, pressure from the Charles Fox-Lord North coalition removed Shelburne in 1783 and Pitt went automatically. The Fox-North coalition was regarded by the general public as a synonym for dishonesty and corruption, so that Pitt's stand against them – a rivalry that lasted a lifetime – earned him the moniker "Honest Billy." None-

theless, "Billy" wasn't above greasing many palms and magnifying reputations through the use of honours. At the age of twenty-four, he became England's youngest ever Prime Minister. At the time, his leadership was expected to be a question of months, hence the popular ditty: "A sight to make nations stand and stare: a kingdom entrusted to a schoolboy's care." Nevertheless, he remained in power for 17 years and sought to bring about a series of financial and social reforms of variable usefulness.

8. Charles James Fox (1749–1806) was a prominent Whig politician who became Britain's first Foreign Secretary in 1782. A dissolute man with expensive tastes, he was already in debt to the tune of £140,000 by the age of twenty five! He became MP for Midhurst in 1768 and was in and out of government throughout his life. He was noted for his support of the French Revolution (probably because of his intense hatred for England's George III), American independence and opposition to slavery.

9. The Adullamites were a short-lived faction that appeared in the British Liberal Party in 1866. Following Lord Palmerston's death the year before, the Liberal Party in general concluded that a second electoral Reform Bill was required. This was opposed, however, by elements within the party which rallied round Robert Lowe and Lord Elcho. They were dubbed "Adullamites" by John Bright. He was alluding to the Cave of Adullam mentioned in the Old Testament where David sought refuge from King Saul. The allusion came to symbolize those who were political outsiders plotting a comeback, or a group dedicated to overthrowing the status quo. In this case, the Adullamites managed to force Lord Russell's resignation, but an attempt at a Conservative-Adullamite alliance came to nothing because of the latter's horror of Benjamin Disraeli as proposed leader.

10. Victor Grayson (1881–circa 1920) was an enigmatic and mercurial political character. After reading socialist journals like *The Clarion, Justice* and *The Labour Leader* for some time, Grayson joined the ILP and  against all the odds–and the expressed opposition of the National Executive of the Labour Party–was elected MP for Colne Valley in 1907. His speaking abilities became well-known, but so too did his drinking problem which made him an increasingly erratic figure. After WWI–and fully in line with the thesis of Belloc and Cecil Chesterton–Grayson attacked the British Prime Minister at a public meeting in Liverpool maintaining that honours were being sold for between £10,000–40,000. He stated: "This sale of honours is a national scandal. It can be traced right down to 10 Downing Street, and to a monocled dandy with offices in Whitehall." The monocled figure referred to was Arthur Maundy Gregory, an MI5 agent and close friend of Sir Basil Thompson, the head of Britain's Special Branch. It was the latter who had Grayson spied upon, so Grayson decided to repay him in kind by spying upon those involved in the honours for sale scandal, a thing made possible by assistance from influential sources. On September 28th, 1920 Grayson was seen entering a house on the Thames Riverbank by an artist friend

who thought nothing about it at the time. Grayson, however, was never seen again. An investigation carried out in the 1960s revealed that the house belonged to Gregory, and it was concluded that Grayson had been captured/murdered there. In 1932, Gregory was convicted of corruption, but was fined a mere £50 and given a suspended two month gaol sentence. He was "persuaded" by the Conservative Party to move to Paris where he was paid a pension of £2,000 p.a. to "keep him sweet."

11. Robert Walpole (1676–1745) was the first Earl of Orford, a zealous Whig politician, and the first unofficial "Prime Minister" of Great Britain. In the early eighteenth century, he became an important member of the Cabinet, but was impeached in 1712 and expelled from the House of Commons. He returned, however, and became the Privy Councillor in the Cabinet dominated by Lord Townsend, his brother-in-law. In 1715, he became Chancellor of the Exchequer and sought ways to deal with Britain's burgeoning National Debt. The government, thereafter, established this proposal: that the South Sea Company would assume the payment of the National Debt in return for lucrative government bonds and concessions. Walpole invested heavily in the company, but the disaster known as the South Sea Bubble ensued. He was saved from financial ruin by his banker in 1720 – though at what price, we do not know. We do know, however, that a 1721 investigation into the Bubble demonstrated widespread corruption in the Cabinet – shades of the later Marconi Scandal. In spite of this, Walpole became the dominant force in government following the death of King George I, with Wikipedia commenting that Walpole made "liberal use of the royal patronage, granting honours and making appointments for political gain."

12. O si sic omnes – "Thus are all men!"

13. Sir William Vernon Harcourt (1827–1904) was a Cambridge-educated barrister who became a Queens Counsel in 1866, and was related to many of the great English families. He sat as a Liberal MP for Oxford from 1868–1880, and for Derby from 1880–1895. He was a member of five Liberal government cabinets during his lifetime. He was made Solicitor-General in 1873 and was knighted the same year. He was Chancellor of the Exchequer from 1892–1895. However, when Lord Rosebery became the Liberal Prime Minister he largely fell out with the direction of the Party which was aiming at Liberal Imperialism. Harcourt often railed against the government and was very critical of the war of aggression and greed launched against the Boer Republics in South Africa.

14. Henry Campbell-Bannerman (1836–1908) was educated at Glasgow and Cambridge universities, and entered Parliament in 1868. A believer in free trade, he was made Financial Secretary to the War Office and then Secretary of State for War in Gladstone's next two governments. He formed a government himself in 1905, remained in office until 1908, and became the first officially designated Prime Minister of Britain. One of his most important acts was the granting of

various government posts to the notoriously corrupt David Lloyd George. At the *numberten.gov.uk* website there is no hint of Campbell-Bannerman's corruption, the PC site preferring to quote "C.B.": "We wish to make the land less of a pleasure ground for the rich and more of a treasure house for the nation." Some might call this rank hypocrisy.

15. The Chinese Labour Problem arose in South Africa because of a deficiency in native labour after the second Boer War. With the ending of the indentured labour scheme, begun in the British Empire in 1842, and the permanent settlement of the imported Indians in the country, the owners of the Rand mines (now under British and Jewish control) enacted an ordinance in 1904 providing for the importation of Chinese labour. The terms were such that the Chinese were little better than slaves. The Boers of the Transvaal greeted this capitalist huckstering with dismay, pointing out that the country's ethnic problems were already complex, without adding a Chinese element to the mix. Their point of view was largely accepted by a British public opinion which viewed the Rand mine owners as little more than gangsters. Nonetheless, between 1904 and 1906, 50,000 Chinese were imported to lower costs and increase profits.

16. One suspects that in respect of the Irish Nationalist Party, CKC and Belloc are being rather too generous. The Nationalists under the leadership of both Charles Parnell and John Redmond had an approach to politics which, in spite of their party name, was very English in its origins: they sought to be all things to all men, and acted accordingly. Gilbert Chesterton grasped this fact more perfectly and in succinct form in the *Illustrated London News*, dated July 20th, 1907 when he said: "The Nationalist MPs at Westminster are represented as fanatics waving firebrands and screaming for massacre. In Ireland they are represented as over-cautious diplomatists effecting a dubious compromise, and occasionally as timid traitors selling their ideal for the comforts of England." One suspects that "selling" is the operative word here.

17. Covent Garden today is an area of central London that is dominated by shopping and entertainment facilities. Its Catholic origins are barely known. During the period of King John in the twelfth century, a 40 acre site was acquired which in due course saw the construction of the Abbey or Convent of St. Peter, Westminster. The Convent maintained a large kitchen garden throughout the Middle Ages and for three centuries "Convent Garden"—as it was originally known—became a major source of fruit and vegetables in London. Post-Reformation, it became known as Covent Garden (probably to hide the fact that the site was plundered by greedy Protestant aristocrats) and operated as a market up until 1974.

18. Cecil John Rhodes (1853–1902) was a Rothschild-linked financier, who was reputed to be one of the richest men of his day. A fanatical advocate of British imperialism, he began his "career" when he was sent to Natal in South Africa

to assist his brother on a cotton farm. The farm's crop failure led the brothers to move to Kimberley where a diamond fever had erupted. By astute manoeuvres, Rhodes had become a millionaire by the age of twenty-five. Returning to Oxford University in the 1870s, he joined the Freemasons–an allegiance that he both maintained and manipulated for his own interests. He became the Prime Minister of the Cape Colony in 1890, and later his name was given to Rhodesia–modern-day Zimbabwe. One of the existing fruits of his lucrative and underhand dealings with farmers in South Africa is the De Beers diamond company, a fruit made possible by his mania for trying to bring the independent Boer Republics under British control.

19. Francis Schnadhorst (1840–1900) was born in Birmingham, England. In 1873, he organised the Birmingham Liberal Association so well that they made large electoral gains in the city. He was requested to replicate his system throughout the country. He established the National Liberal Federation in 1877 and, as its first Secretary, he greatly aided Liberal Party General Election victories in 1880, 1885 and 1892. In 1897, in recognition of his services to the Liberal Party, he received £10,000 guineas–a sum equivalent to hundreds of thousands of pounds today! One of the "services" provided appeared in 1891. Schnadhorst "found" two gentlemen–Sydney Stern and James Williamson–who were willing to buy peerages. Gladstone, as Prime Minister, agreed. Money changed hands and both were "ennobled" in 1895. The *Irish Student Law Review* notes: "What Gladstone saw as a temporary expedient became by the 1900s a normal incident of political life . . . . and Lloyd George was the first Prime Minister to set fees for the sale of honours, which were publicly revealed by the Duke of Northumberland on July 17th, 1922 in the House of Lords."

20. The Cecil family made their name and fortune in Elizabethan England when William Cecil, Lord Burghley, and his son Robert, Earl of Salisbury, persuaded, cajoled and manipulated Elizabeth I to maintain a persistent, violent anti-Catholic policy throughout her reign. Along with other families, the Cecils looted Church property on a grandiose scale and built an intricate network of spies and intelligence-gatherers throughout the country and beyond. This network, combined with their unlimited ambition and cunning, ensured their victory over other factions of the day, both Catholic and Dissenter. The family is to this day immensely rich and influential.

21. The Corn Laws existed in England between 1815 and 1846. Ostensibly they were tariffs to protect British agriculture–overwhelmingly dominated by the aristocratic class–from cheap foreign grain imports. Opposition to this tax coalesced around the Anti-Corn Law League which was founded in 1839 and was openly the mouthpiece of rising industrial capitalism in the country. Its arguments were founded on the theories of the Jewish economist, David Ricardo, who maintained that if grain prices were lowered, the industrial magnates could lower wages and increase their profits. As part of the League's campaign, they

assisted in the publication of *The Economist*, a magazine which has been a faithful servant of capitalism ever since.

22. Beatrice Webb (née Potter) was a British socialist, economist and reformer who married Sidney Webb who–in spite of his alleged hatred of class privilege–was content to become Baron Passfield in 1929. Potter and her husband worked as a team and were both founders and organisers of the Fabian Society and the ultra-progressive London School of Economics. A co-founder of the socialist journal, *The New Statesman*, in 1913, she also co-authored books like *The History of Trade Unionism* (1894) and *Soviet Communism: A New Civilization?* (1935). In spite of a few feeble caveats, the latter book was an exercise in mendacity of grotesque proportions which whitewashed the many crimes of Stalin.

23. Frederick Edwin Smith (1872–1930) was an Oxford-educated barrister who entered Parliament as a Conservative in 1906. In 1915 he was appointed Solicitor-General by Asquith and later in the year as Attorney-General. In 1919 he was created Baron Birkenhead and in 1922 Earl of Birkenhead. From 1924–1928 he was the Secretary of State for India. Churchill's closest friend, he was a renowned orator but what he propounded was often absurd. He was famously lampooned by Gilbert Chesterton in the poem, "The Reunion of Christendom."

24. John Redmond (1856–1918) was a barrister drawn from the Catholic gentry of Ireland. He entered Parliament as MP for New Ross in 1880, and demonstrated great flair as an orator, though he always showed himself to be a committed parliamentarian–something that most Irish found repugnant as time went on. This should have come as no surprise for in spite of the ban of the Catholic hierarchy on attendance at (Protestant) Trinity University in Dublin (a ban instituted because it threatened Catholic values at their roots), he chose to study there. He came to the leadership of the Nationalist Party in 1900, following the Parnell crisis and the subsequent years of intra-party squabbling. His aim at Westminster was to secure Irish Home Rule and, on paper, this was achieved. It passed in the House of Commons but its implementation was suspended until the end of WWI. The 1916 Irish Republican Rebellion put an end to that compromise as well as to Redmond's brand of politics. To the Republican demand for complete opposition to conscription in Ireland, Redmond encouraged recruitment to the British Army; to the Republican demand for Irish independence, Redmond sought Irish loyalty within the British Empire. Redmond's politics and party broke down on those points and by the time of Redmond's death the Nationalist Party was effectively dead and buried.

25. Frederick Jowett (1864–1944) was a Christian socialist who got involved in politics in 1886 through the Socialist League. His primary inspiration was William Morris whom he had read as a youth. He was the first socialist elected to Bradford City Council in 1892 whereupon he founded the growing Independent Labour Party in the city. At his insistence the city was the first in the country to

provide free school meals. He entered Parliament in 1906, and became Chairman of the ILP in 1909. In the *Socialist Review*, Jowett called for the Cabinet system to be abolished and replaced with committees representing all parties so that more power was exercised by individual MPs. He was appointed Commissioner of Works in 1924 under Ramsey MacDonald. He shared a certain fellow-feeling with people like Belloc and GKC because of his fervent opposition to the Boer War.

# Titles New & Old from IHS Press
## are available direct from the publisher or at fine bookstores.

*The Outline of Sanity,* by G.K. Chesterton
184pp, 6"x9", ISBN 0-9714894-0-8, Item No. GKC001 **$14.95**

*The Free Press,* by Hilaire Belloc
96pp, 5½"x8½", ISBN 0-9714894-1-6, Item No. HB001 **$8.95**

*Action: A Manual for the Reconstruction of Christendom,* by Jean Ousset
272pp, 6"x9", ISBN 0-9714894-2-4, Item No. JO001 **$16.95**

*An Essay on the Restoration of Property,* by Hilaire Belloc
104pp, 5½"x8½", ISBN 0-9714894-4-0, Item No. HB002 **$8.95**

*Utopia of Usurers,* by G.K. Chesterton
136pp, 5½"x8½", ISBN 0-9714894-3-2, Item No. GKC002 **$11.95**

*Irish Impressions,* by G.K. Chesterton
152pp, 5½"x8½", ISBN 0-9714894-5-9, Item No. GKC003 **$12.95**

*The Church and the Land,* by Fr. Vincent McNabb
192pp, 6"x9", ISBN 0-9714894-6-7, Item No. VM001 **$14.95**

*Capitalism, Protestantism and Catholicism,* by Amintore Fanfani
192pp, 6"x9", ISBN 0-9714894-7-5, Item No. AF001 **$14.95**

*Twelve Types,* by G.K. Chesterton
96pp, 5½"x8½", ISBN 0-9714894-8-3, Item No. GKC004 **$8.95**

*The Gauntlet: A Challenge to the Myth of Progress,* A first anthology of the writings of Arthur J. Penty
96pp, 5½"x8½", ISBN 0-9714894-9-1, Item No. AP001 **$8.95**

*Flee to the Fields,* the papers of the Catholic Land Movement
160pp, 5½"x8½", ISBN 0-9718286-0-1, Item No. FF001 **$12.95**

*An Essay on the Economic Effects of the Reformation,* by George O'Brien
160pp, 5½"x8½", ISBN 0-9718286-2-8, Item No. GO001 **$12.95**

*Charles I,* by Hilaire Belloc
288pp, 6"x9", ISBN 0-9718286-3-6, Item No. HB003 **$16.95**

*Charles II: the Last Rally,* by Hilaire Belloc
224pp, 6"x9", ISBN 0-9718286-4-4, Item No. HB004 **$15.95**

*A Miscellany of Men,* by G.K. Chesterton
184pp, 5½"x8½", ISBN 0-9718286-1-X, Item No. GKC005 **$13.95**

*Distributist Perspectives,* Vol. I, by the chief Distibutists
96pp, 5½"x8½", ISBN 0-9718286-7-9, Item No. DP001 **$8.95**

*Dollfuss: An Austrian Patriot,* by Fr. Johannes Messner
160pp, 5½"x8½", ISBN 0-9718286-6-0, Item No. JM001 **$12.95**

*Economics for Helen,* by Hilaire Belloc
160pp, 5½"x8½", ISBN 1-932528-03-2, Item No. HB006 **$12.95**

*Richelieu,* by Hilaire Belloc
272pp, 6"x9", ISBN 0-9718286-8-7, Item No. HB005 **$16.95**

*The Guild State,* by G. R. S. Taylor
128pp, 5½"x8½", ISBN 1-932528-00-8, Item No. GT001 **$11.95**

*Neo-CONNED!,* by Pat Buchanan, Jude Wanniski, Sam Francis, et al
447pp, 6"x9", ISBN 1-932528-04-0, Item No. NC01 **$19.95** (paperback)

*Neo-CONNED! Again,* by Robert Fisk, Robert Hickson, Donn de Grand Pré, et al
897pp, 6"x9", ISBN 1-932528-05-9, Item No. NC02 **$29.95** (paperback)

**Order direct today:** by phone, fax, mail, e-mail, online.
**s/h:** $3.50 per book; $1.50 ea. add'l. book. Check, m.o., VISA, MC.

*toll-free telephone or fax:* 877-IHS-PRES (877.447.7737)
*e-mail:* order@ihspress.com • *internet:* www.ihspress.com

# About IHS Press

IHS Press believes that the key to the restoration of Catholic Society is the recovery and the implementation of the wisdom our Fathers in the Faith possessed so fully less than a century ago. At a time when numerous ideologies were competing for supremacy, these men articulated, with precision and vigor, and *without* apology or compromise, the only genuine alternative to the then- (and still-) prevailing currents of thought: value-free and yet bureaucratic "progressivism" on the one hand, and the rehashed, *laissez-faire* free-for-all of "conservatism" on the other. That alternative is the Social Teaching of the Catholic Church.

Catholic Social Teaching offers the solutions to the political, economic, and social problems that plague modern society; problems that stem from the false principles of the Reformation, Renaissance, and Revolution, and which are exacerbated by the industrialization and the secularization of society that has continued for several centuries. Defending, explaining, and applying this Teaching was the business of the great Social Catholics of last century. Unfortunately, much of their work is today both unknown and unavailable.

Thus, IHS Press was founded in September of 2001A.D. as the only publisher dedicated exclusively to the Social Teaching of the Church, helping Catholics of the third millennium pick up where those of last century left off. IHS Press is committed to recovering, and *helping others to rediscover*, the valuable works of the Catholic economists, historians, and social critics. To that end, IHS Press is in the business of issuing critical editions of works on society, politics, and economics by writers, thinkers, and men of action such as Hilaire Belloc, Gilbert Chesterton, Arthur Penty, Fr. Vincent McNabb, Fr. Denis Fahey, Jean Ousset, Amintore Fanfani, George O'Brien, and others, making the wisdom they contain available to the current generation.

It is the aim of IHS Press to issue these vitally important works in high-quality volumes and at reasonable prices, to enable the widest possible audience to acquire, enjoy, and benefit from them. Such an undertaking cannot be maintained without the support of generous benefactors. With that in mind, IHS Press was constituted as a not-for-profit corporation which is exempt from federal tax according to Section 501(c)(3) of the United States Internal Revenue Code. Donations to IHS Press are, therefore, tax deductible, and are especially welcome to support its continued operation, and to help it with the publication of new titles and the more widespread dissemination of those already in print.

For more information, contact us at:

*mail:* 222 W. 21ˢᵗ St., Suite F-122~Norfolk, VA 23517 USA
*toll-free telephone or fax:* 877-IHS-PRES (877.447.7737)
*e-mail:* order@ihspress.com • *internet:* www.ihspress.com

IHS Press is a tax-exempt 501(c)(3) corporation; EIN: 54-2057581.
Applicable documentation is available upon request.